BRADLEY WIGGINS

The Story of Britain's Greatest-Ever Cyclist

First published by Carlton Books Ltd in 2012

Carlton Books Ltd
20 Mortimer Street
London W1T 3JW

**PRESS
ASSOCIATION**
Sport

A CIP catalogue record for this book is available from the
British Library.

ISBN 978-1-78097-310-4

Printed in Germany

BRADLEY WIGGINS

The Story of Britain's Greatest-Ever Cyclist

FOREWORD BY CHRIS BOARDMAN MBE

Matt McGeehan

CARLTON

CONTENTS

BORN RACER

1

NEW KID

2

GREEK DRAMA

3

ROAD TRIP

4

'I have been told I was an inspiration for him. It is very generous of him, but now he's the inspiration for all of us. He's the greatest British cyclist ever.'
— Chris Boardman on Bradley Wiggins

FOREWORD

CHRIS BOARDMAN MBE

I'd like to say thank you to Bradley Wiggins, because he got me back into cycling. After ending my career, I spent time doing everything I couldn't do as a professional. Then I received a phone call from my former coach, and then performance director of British Cycling, Peter Keen. Peter was asking for my advice. He had a young rider who, having made a strong start to his track career, wanted to go professional on the road as I had done.

I had a word with Brad and asked him to write down, in an email, what he wanted to achieve and how he was going to do it. I used red font for my comments – it was as if I was marking his homework – and within two exchanges, we had established a clear career path for him. I certainly don't want to credit myself with having any impact on his career, it was just a conversation. He's totally his own man and a very smart guy; there's a lot going on in his head which doesn't come out of his mouth. He has always had the physical ability and technique. I can remember standing next to him once doing a roller warm-up and you could hear the increase in power through the rollers but hardly see any change at all in his body movement. There was almost none. Movement is waste and it showed he was getting the absolute most out of his muscles in a technique which has served him well.

I have been told I was an inspiration for him. It is very generous of him, but now he's the inspiration for all of us. He's the greatest British cyclist ever. Even Sir Chris Hoy would recognise that. Brad's got the breadth – from 4km to 3,500km. Only one person can become the first British Tour de France champion, so his achievement cannot be surpassed. He has taken British cycling into a new era.

The biggest challenge he had to overcome was himself. The people around him supported him and, to Brad's credit, he listened and accepted responsibility. He handled all the expectation to win the Tour and then, in front of a worldwide audience, he said: 'We're just going to draw the raffle numbers now.' I like that. I like his character and the emotional outbursts, because it shows he's a real person. I'm not sure about the sideburns, though.

Chris Boardman won Great Britain's first Olympic cycling gold medal for 72 years with victory in the 4km individual pursuit at the 1992 Games in Barcelona. The Wirral rider transferred from track to road, winning the Tour de France prologue on three occasions and wearing the race leader's yellow jersey for a total of five days. He was British Cycling's head of research and development at the 2008 and 2012 Olympic Games and worked as a commentator for ITV and BBC as Bradley Wiggins won the Tour de France and Olympic time-trial gold in 2012.

> 'Some dreams do come true. My old mother over there,
> her son's just won the Tour de France.'
> – Bradley Wiggins in 2012

INTRODUCTION

Bradley Wiggins, the 'Kid from Kilburn', achieved sporting immortality in the summer of 2012, becoming the first British winner of the Tour de France before winning Olympic gold in London.

ABOVE Every cyclist's dream, standing on top of the podium on the Champs-Elysées.

OPPOSITE The extraordinary summer of 2012 is completed by time-trial gold at the London Olympics.

His is an extraordinary story: from Herne Hill Velodrome to the Olympic Velodrome, Hayes by-pass to Hampton Court Palace, solitary rides over Lancashire hills to leading the peloton over Pyrenean peaks and Alpine summits at the Tour de France.

Wiggins is six times a world champion, four times an Olympic champion and the first Briton to win the Tour's fabled yellow jersey, achievements Sir Chris Hoy believes are impossible to surpass.

With sporting fever building towards the London 2012 Olympics, Britain was distracted by events on the Continent as a 32-year-old tattooed Mod with long sideburns, who looked like Rodney Trotter (his own description), won the greatest bike race of them all with a near-flawless display.

On the podium in Paris, with thousands of jubilant Britons waving Union flags, Wiggins performed as he had done on the bike, with panache, thanking his mother Linda who brought him up alone in London.

'We're just going to draw the raffle numbers now,' he joked. More seriously, he added: 'It's been a magical couple of weeks. Some dreams do come true. My old mother over there, her son's just won the Tour de France.'

The self-confessed cycling recluse, a music aficionado, lover of Liverpool Football Club and Wigan Rugby League, fine mimic and king of the one-liners, received the acclaim of the nation.

He then had the expectation of the country on his shoulders at London 2012, but still delivered victory in the road time-trial at Hampton Court, as his journey to greatness was completed just a few miles from where he was brought up.

He said: 'Winning the Tour and then winning Olympic gold in London... it is never, ever going to get any better than that. It's been an amazing six weeks.'

He took to his bike after being inspired, 20 years earlier, by 1992 Olympic individual pursuit winner Chris Boardman and five-time Tour champion Miguel Indurain. Wiggins has

used his prodigious talent to the full, transforming himself from track thoroughbred and Olympic champion in Beijing in 2008 to winning the toughest endurance event in sport four years later.

He has achieved every target he has set himself, leading the way for British cycling on the track and the open road for the next generation, who can follow in his revolutions in a bid to emulate his success.

'I'm just a kid from London who happened to be good at cycling,' he said. 'I don't want to be a role model as a person, because I'm only human at the end of the day; I make mistakes. In a sporting sense, fire away. Love me to bits. It's nice because you are actually doing something with your life that is inspirational. Someone will be inspired out there and the great thing about cycling is anyone can go and ride that circuit and pretend they're one of us.'

Wiggins plans to be a part of the sport for some time to come. He said: 'I love cycling. I come from a cycling family. I'll probably be there in 20 years' time marshalling on the corner somewhere for a local 10km. I'll always be riding my bike.'

BORN RACER

A 15-year-old Bradley Wiggins receives the National Juvenile Points trophy from former Tour de France stage winner Sean Yates.

> **'I am half-Australian whether you like it or not. But I'm very much British. I grew up with my mother and not my father.'**
> – Wiggins describes his background

BORN RACER

Bradley Wiggins was destined to race a bike. His parents, Linda and Gary, married in January 1979 after meeting at the Paddington track in west London. Gary had travelled to Europe from Australia, seeking to make a living from riding in city centre criterium races and competing in velodromes across the continent.

Wiggins was born on April 28, 1980 in Ghent, where Gary was based while racing on the six-day circuit, but he was drinking as hard as he was racing and Linda was often on the receiving end of his rage.

Wiggins and his mother returned to London at the end of 1982, the relationship with Gary over. On one visit to the UK soon afterwards, Gary insisted on taking Wiggins to London Zoo, a photograph from the trip providing one of the few snapshots of Wiggins with his father. A few weeks later a child's bike arrived, but Wiggins did not see his father again for 14 years and even then the relationship was fleeting.

Years later, Wiggins was asked if he considered what his father would have thought of his successes. It was not something he was prepared to ponder for long. 'I don't know, it's difficult to say,' Wiggins said. 'It depends if he was sober. I've put that one to bed.' He acknowledged his father's influence and his bloodline. 'I am half-Australian whether you like it or not,' he said. 'But I'm very much British. I grew up with my mother and not my father.' Wiggins and his mother initially returned to her family home and his grandparents, George and

LEFT The 15-year-old Wiggins wins the juvenile race at a Paddington CC event at Eastway circuit in London in 1995.

BELOW LEFT AND RIGHT The exploits of Miguel Indurain and Chris Boardman fired Wiggins' imagination.

'Every kid when I was a kid used to kick a football round, pretend they were Gary Lineker or Paul Gascoigne; they were in the FA Cup. I used to come and ride around in lycra as a 12-year-old and get it taken out of me.'
– Wiggins on his early passion for race cycling

Maureen, had a strong influence on his upbringing. George was the father figure Gary failed to be and took Wiggins to greyhound racing across London and to the British Legion to play darts, pool and cards.

Wiggins was one of the wise-cracking children in class at school, lacking application and making mischief, but he was good at sport, including football.

Tottenham and Arsenal were well-supported among his contemporaries and Wiggins once knocked on Gary Lineker's door after discovering where the England striker lived. He was given a signed photograph by Lineker's then wife and ushered away. Despite that brush with superstardom, cycling was beginning to have a greater influence.

The 1989 Tour de France, won by Greg LeMond by eight seconds from Laurent Fignon, had an early impact, but it was an event three years later which would have a more gripping effect.

On Wednesday, July 29, 1992, Chris Boardman was riding in the 4km individual pursuit final in Barcelona, seeking Britain's first Olympic cycling gold medal in 72 years. Aware of the potential for history to be made and keen for Wiggins to see an event in which his father competed, his mum called him in from playing football with friends.

His eyes were transfixed on the screen as Boardman, riding his futuristic Lotus bike with carbon-fibre frame and disc wheels, and wearing his black aerodynamic helmet, finished victorious, winning Britain's first gold medal of the 1992 Olympic Games.

He became gripped by Olympic fever and after every British success – be it Boardman, Linford Christie in the 100m on the athletics track or rowers Steve Redgrave and Matthew Pinsent – he would take to his bike and ride around the block of flats he called home, imagining himself competing in the Games.

Spaniard Miguel Indurain, who won his first of five consecutive Tour titles in 1991, was also an early hero for Wiggins. He would set up a turbo-trainer in the sitting room of the flat he shared with his mother, riding on the rollers as he watched the Tour, pretending he was part of the peloton. The exotic race, with few Brits competing, had an intoxicating allure and Wiggins was hooked.

He began riding his bike everywhere and soon ventured further afield, circling Hyde Park, away from the traffic, and imagining he was in the Tour de France, while his friends were playing football, picturing themselves at Wembley and lifting the FA Cup.

'Every kid when I was a kid used to kick a football round, pretend they were Gary Lineker or Paul Gascoigne; they were in the FA Cup,' Wiggins said. 'I used to come and ride around in lycra as a 12-year-old and get it taken out of me.'

Encouraged by Linda, Wiggins joined a local cycling club, riding on the Hayes by-pass and at Herne Hill Velodrome, a venue where his father once raced. 'My mother took me out there and I started racing and I finished third, and we went back the week after and I won it,' he said. 'Then you just go from there and before you know it, you're competing at national level.'

His talent was evident almost immediately, but there were setbacks and he fractured a collarbone after going over his handlebars in rush-hour traffic. Wiggins' mother pursued compensation from the driver and won, the sum awarded contributing to a new racing bike.

Wiggins' interest in the Tour was heightened when he travelled to Paris with his mother in 1993. They stood behind a set of railings before the entrance to the Place de la Concorde, around a kilometre from the finish line on the Champs-Elysées, as Indurain rode to a third yellow jersey. It was Wiggins' first sight of the Tour peloton and further stoked his desire to one day join it.

Racing and training became the routine for Wiggins, who won numerous national titles and quickly attracted the attention of coaches and selectors. After setting records in events including the 1km time-trial and the individual

BELOW LEFT The 16-year-old Wiggins in the colours of Archer Road Club at the Manchester velodrome.

BELOW RIGHT Wiggins wearing the rainbow jersey of the world junior champion for the 2km individual pursuit, which he won in Cuba in 1997.

pursuit, as well as winning points and scratch mass bunch races, he was invited to Manchester for training weekends. He became a self-confessed cycling recluse; nothing else mattered. He declined the usual teenage pursuits – parties, girls and football – to focus on riding his bike.

His studies were also secondary and he left school to devote more time to training and racing, later returning to have a conversation in fluent French with a teacher who was convinced he was a lost cause. Wiggins' language skills had been acquired on the road, rather than from a textbook.

To help fund his pursuit, he was employed as a kitchen hand at the Cumberland Hotel, pot washing and cutting vegetables, and had another job as a carpenter at the Lanesborough Hotel, but he rarely lasted long in employment.

He enrolled in a BTEC business studies course, but left that after excusing himself to represent Great Britain at a competition in Denmark in January 1997; his decision to focus on cycling appeared justified when later that year he won a gold medal at the Junior Track Cycling World Championships in Cuba.

It was clear Wiggins was a prodigious talent and his ability was recognised further when he became the first Lottery-funded cyclist on the world-class performance programme run by Peter Keen. Keen had coached Boardman to his Barcelona gold medal, and now Wiggins was set to start a new Lottery-funded era.

Wiggins travelled to the 1998 Commonwealth Games in Kuala Lumpur, aged 18, to compete in the individual and team pursuit events. He was fourth in the individual competition, but won silver in the four-man event as Australia won gold.

The adventure had started with a medal in his first major Games as the British Cycling revolution was beginning, with Wiggins to the fore. The Sydney Olympic Games, the Track Cycling World Championships in Manchester and the beginnings of a road career in France were imminent.

London was still home, but Wiggins was beginning to put down roots in Lancashire after being attracted to a girl he had met in British Cycling's junior set-up.

After a slow beginning to the courtship, Wiggins plucked up the courage to ask the sprinter out.

'I probably wouldn't be where I am in cycling if I hadn't met Cath,' Wiggins said. 'It gave me that base to really think about what's important.'

LEFT Wiggins (middle) won Commonwealth Games silver in Kuala Lumpur in 1998 at the age of 18 as part of England's team pursuit squad.

RIGHT In one of his earliest senior competitions for Great Britain, Wiggins (top) won silver in the team pursuit at the 2000 track World Championships in Manchester.

NEW KID

Wiggins' first Olympic medal came in the team pursuit with Paul Manning, Chris Newton and Bryan Steele at Sydney 2000.

> **'When it happens it's quite a strange emotion, something I can't explain. It's just a relief more than anything.'**
> – Wiggins on becoming a world champion for the first time

NEW KID

Eight years on from watching Chris Boardman ride to Olympic gold from his mother's sitting room, Bradley Wiggins travelled to the 2000 Games in Sydney. He was a member of the Great Britain team which also included Boardman, who was set to ride in the road time-trial.

On Monday, September 18, 2000, two days after Jason Queally had made a spectacular start to the Games with victory in the 1km time-trial, Wiggins became an Olympian at the Dunc Gray Velodrome.

The 20-year-old joined Paul Manning, Chris Newton and Bryan Steel for the 4km team pursuit as the British quartet clocked an Olympic record of 4 minutes 4.030 seconds to advance to the next round as fastest qualifiers.

Later that same day, the British squad met Russia in the quarter-finals, catching their rivals and progressing, but the contest for medals was close and their time from the morning session was bettered by three teams.

Rob Hayles and Jonny Clay were drafted in for Steel and Newton for the following day's semi-finals, but Wiggins and his team-mates were beaten as Ukraine advanced to the gold medal ride-off in a new world record of 4 minutes 0.834 seconds.

Britain, with Steel and Newton back in the line-up, responded with a convincing win in the battle for bronze with France, lowering their own best time to 4 minutes 1.979 seconds, before Germany became the first team to go beneath the four-minute barrier in winning gold. Wiggins played a full part in Britain's fourth track cycling medal of the Games, but

LEFT Team pursuit silver in 2000 was Wiggins' first medal at a senior World Championships.

BELOW On the podium in Sydney after earning bronze in the Olympic team pursuit.

'Bradley and me are good at this type of racing and we want to be back in four years and get what we should have won.'
– Rob Hayles on crashing in the Madison in Sydney

not everyone was happy. Hayles and Clay had not fulfilled the criteria to be awarded medals and could not join their team-mates on the podium, receiving medals only after an appeal by the British Olympic Association. Hayles also believed he could have helped Britain into the gold medal ride-off, saying: 'I was sure we could give the Germans a run for their money.'

Hayles, who narrowly missed out on individual pursuit bronze, had a busy programme and was joined by Wiggins for the Madison as the two-man event, where riders slingshot each other into the action, made its Olympic debut on the sixth and final day of track competition.

It was an eventful 240-lap (60km) race for the British pair, who won the first and third sprints to share the lead with Australia at the halfway mark. Australia's Brett Aitken and Scott McGrory moved into the lead alone by scoring more consistently than the Britons, who were second with 20 laps to go, equal on 13 points with Italy's Marco Villa and Silvio Martinello. Wiggins put in one final acceleration before handing over to Hayles for the finishing sprint. Hayles was battling for position on the penultimate lap when he was involved in a collision, hitting the track hard, effectively ending hopes of another British medal.

Belgium and Italy scored well at the finish and Wiggins and Hayles had to settle for fourth place behind Australia. 'It was like slow motion as I went down,' Hayles said. 'I just couldn't believe this was happening to me. There was a silver medal to go for and a certainty of bronze at least. This has been the best week of my life and yet I'm coming away with two fourths and a third. I'd have settled for that total a few months ago, but now I want more. I feel robbed.'

Hayles had faith in his partnership with Wiggins and vowed to respond from the setback. He said: 'Bradley and me are good at this type of racing and we want to be back in four years and get what we should have won.'

Wiggins returned from Sydney to win a first senior World Championships medal, claiming team pursuit silver in Manchester in October 2000. His potential on the road was also beginning to be recognised, and in November 2000 he signed his first professional contract with the Linda McCartney Racing Team. The team had lofty goals and was continuing despite the death from cancer of Linda, wife of Beatle Sir Paul McCartney, early in the project. They had become the first British team to ride in the Giro d'Italia but uncertainty was growing over the sustainability of the team, which included Sean Yates, the second Briton to wear the Tour de France's yellow jersey, and Max Sciandri, the Anglo-Italian who won road race bronze at the 1996 Atlanta Olympics.

Linda McCartney Foods was the title sponsor but was used mainly to recruit other brands, and rumours of interest from Jaguar and Jacob's Creek wines never fully materialised.

Wiggins had moved to Toulouse to begin his Continental career and travelled to London for the team's season launch, only to discover from Sciandri and Yates that funds had dried up and the team was being disbanded. Wiggins, who was yet to turn 21, took the news in his stride, returning to the British team and refocusing on the track.

Wiggins was feeling better than ever as the 2001 Track Cycling World Championships approached, but two weeks ahead of the competition in Antwerp, Belgium, he suffered a setback following a freak accident.

He was riding along Harrow Road in west London when a gust of wind blew a tarpaulin which had been covering a skip into his path. The tarpaulin snagged in his handlebars and Wiggins was propelled forward, suffering a fractured wrist which required an operation.

Wiggins raced at the World Championships with a plaster cast on his arm and advanced from individual pursuit qualifying before being eliminated.

'It didn't go as well as I had hoped, although when I lay on the operating table I never thought I'd be here competing,' Wiggins said. 'It's been a difficult two weeks since the operation. It wasn't so much the injury itself as the fact that

I missed time doing speed training. It put me back six or seven days.'

There were happy times in Antwerp, though, as Wiggins claimed a silver medal in the team pursuit, alongside Manning, Newton and Steel, behind Ukraine. He also agreed a deal with the Française des Jeux squad sponsored by the French national lottery.

He said: 'To ride with a top professional team is what I always wanted. Having a professional contract has certainly helped my morale, even if it has not cured my wrist.'

Wiggins packed his Ford Fiesta and drove to Nantes to resume the road career which had stalled by the demise of the Linda McCartney team, but he was thrown in at the deep end and isolated in western France. He was keen to make an impression, but struggled in the early part of the season and, as his team-mates prepared for the 2002 Tour de France, Wiggins returned to Manchester ahead of the Commonwealth Games.

There he met a familiar face, Australian Brad McGee. McGee won stage seven of the Tour de France before travelling to Manchester seeking to win the Commonwealth Games individual pursuit title Wiggins also coveted.

The Française des Jeux team-mates met in the final and, despite the roar of a partisan crowd, Wiggins was a distant second best as McGee passed him en route to setting a Commonwealth record and taking Games gold.

Wiggins said: 'It was always going to be difficult going up against Brad. And it was always going to be very difficult mentally because we're friends. Once I sensed he was catching me, my head just went and that was it.'

Manning finished third and Wiggins vowed England would claim revenge in the team pursuit, which McGee skipped due to his hectic schedule.

His confidence proved to be misplaced as Australia won their seventh event out of eight on the track in a world record time, completing the 16 laps in three minutes 59.583 seconds.

'It didn't go as well as I had hoped, although when I lay on the operating table I never thought I'd be here competing.'
– Wiggins on going to the 2001 World Championships after breaking his wrist

TOP LEFT Wiggins won the 2001 team pursuit world silver medal with Chris Newton, Paul Manning and Bryan Steel.

LEFT Wiggins' plaster cast is visible as he stands on the podium.

ABOVE On the track during the individual pursuit at the 2002 Commonwealth Games in Manchester.

RIGHT Celebrating a Commonwealth Games record in the individual pursuit, which friend and rival Brad McGee promptly broke again in the very next race.

Wiggins, who had teamed up with Manning, Newton and Steel, had few complaints. He said. 'I've been beaten twice by two world-class performances. It's been a bit disappointing but when you get beaten by a world record, there's not a lot you can do.'

The 2002 World Championships in Copenhagen followed in September, but Wiggins was unable to exact revenge, placing fifth in the individual pursuit, before claiming bronze in the team event. He had a psychological block where McGee was concerned.

British Cycling recognised Wiggins was not making the expected progress as the 2004 Olympics approached and a meeting was called, led by performance director Peter Keen. Keen decided Wiggins needed help and called in a favour from Boardman, who had retired from racing.

Keen and his fellow senior figures at British Cycling, including Dave Brailsford and Shane Sutton, knew Wiggins' potential was enormous and, having achieved what Wiggins was aiming to do, Boardman was one of the few people who could make Wiggins listen.

Boardman set about the task in meticulous fashion, writing down conversations, helping Wiggins determine his proposed route to defeating McGee on the track and to success on the road. 'I'm on the outside so I have a broader overview,' Boardman said. 'I just ask questions and push them in the right direction.'

Though Wiggins had abandoned the British training regime for life with Française des Jeux, Boardman convinced him to return to the programme that had taken him to the verge of being the leading pursuit rider in the world.

He was also beginning to find happiness away from racing. Wiggins was reacquainted with Cath at the Commonwealth Games and moved in with her as she finished her degree in Manchester, ending his exile in France.

Wiggins' rediscovered focus was rewarded with his first Grand Tour ride in the 2003 Giro d'Italia, but he made little impression. He was one of 34 riders eliminated from the race after failing to complete the 18th stage from Santuario di Vicoforte to Chianale within the time limit. His participation enhanced his endurance, though, and he felt the benefits later in the season.

The 2003 Track Cycling World Championships took place in Stuttgart, Germany after being moved from Shenzhen, China amid concerns over the SARS virus.

Wiggins was the fastest qualifier for the individual pursuit by more than four seconds in 4 minutes 17.342 seconds, the quickest time since Boardman's 'Superman' position, with outstretched arms, was outlawed by the International Cycling Union.

A day later, on Thursday, July 31, 2003, Wiggins lived up to the qualifying ranking by winning a first world champion's rainbow jersey, completing the 16 laps in 4 minutes 18.576 seconds, more than half a second ahead of Australia's Luke Roberts.

Wiggins had hoped to win by a more convincing margin, but was pleased to claim a first world title, even if the enormity of the result was tempered by the absence of McGee.

Wiggins said: 'When it happens it's quite a strange emotion, something I can't explain. It's just a relief more than anything. I thought I'd have a bit more in the tank than him, but that's the pursuit.'

LEFT Wiggins on the track in Stuttgart on his way to the first senior world title of his career in the individual pursuit at the 2003 World Championships.

ABOVE Wearing the world champion's rainbow jersey for the first time, flanked by runner-up Luke Roberts of Australia (left) and third-placed Sergi Escobar of Spain.

ATHENS

Wiggins' first Olympic gold medal came in the individual pursuit in Athens, where he beat Australian Brad McGee.

2004

3

GREEK DRAMA

> **'This team is going to Athens with a possibility of bringing back seven or eight medals.'**
>
> – Wiggins on the eve of the 2004 Olympics

GREEK DRAMA

Olympic year arrived with Bradley Wiggins a world champion for the first time, but he was struggling to build on the success. He was enjoying himself on and off the track and his physical condition was poor when the New Year dawned.

He faced competition from Rob Hayles, Paul Manning and David Millar to secure one of the two individual pursuit spots in Athens, and was far from assured of a place despite his rainbow jersey. With coaches and mentors, including Chris Boardman, trying to rouse Wiggins from his slump, he was 'diplomatically rested' from the 2004 Track Cycling World Championships in Melbourne after finishing behind Manning at a Revolution meeting in April.

The competition was in late May, just two months before Wiggins was hoping to depart for Greece. Wiggins, who had spent the early part of the season focusing on the road with his Credit Agricole team, was confident of peaking at the right time, but there was little evidence to give weight to his optimism.

Ahead of the Olympic selection meeting, he was given a chance to prove himself and his form, but pulled out after six of the 16 laps of an individual pursuit trial. The prospect of missing out on a place in his favoured event at the Games all of a sudden seemed very real.

Shane Sutton was a member of the selection panel and was adamant Wiggins was among Britain's best gold medal hopes for Athens. Manning, fifth in Melbourne, had belief in Wiggins too, so much so that he withdrew his name from the shortlist for the individual event.

The decision to go with Wiggins was further justified when in June Millar, who had to withdraw from the Manchester Track World Cup in April after his Cofidis team opted to suspend competing in response to drugs allegations, admitted to using banned blood-booster erythropoietin (EPO).

Yet Wiggins still had to deliver. After June's Tour of Switzerland his complete attention turned to the track and, slowly but surely, he found his form returning and he began to hit the required numbers in training to ease his own concerns and satisfy the selectors that their decision was correct.

Britain's cyclists decamped to Newport for final Olympic preparations, with Wiggins confident. 'This team is going

LEFT Wiggins kisses his first Olympic gold medal after success in the individual pursuit at the 2004 Games in Athens.

ABOVE David Millar was out of the equation when he admitted use of the banned blood-boosting agent EPO.

'When Cath told me she was pregnant, all the doubts turned to supreme confidence. I was about to do it for someone else.'
– Wiggins on the impact
of impending fatherhood

to Athens with a possibility of bringing back seven or eight medals,' he said.

Wiggins appeared set to play a key part after qualifying in an Olympic record of four minutes 15.165 seconds, knocking more than three seconds off the previous best mark on the opening day of competition in the Olympic Velodrome.

Wiggins' state of mind had been transformed by his partner Cath's revelation that she was expecting; he was going to be a father. 'When Cath told me she was pregnant, all the doubts turned to supreme confidence,' he said later. 'I was about to do it for someone else. I was going out to win a gold medal and get financial security.'

The confidence he exuded spilled on to the track and Wiggins made sure rival Brad McGee was fully aware, winking at his rival after leaving the track following his qualifying ride before the Australian advanced more than two seconds behind his rival.

Chris Hoy then won 1km time-trial gold, inheriting the title Jason Queally claimed in Sydney four years earlier, before Wiggins guaranteed himself a medal by advancing to the final against McGee.

Twenty-four hours later Wiggins was eager to return to battle, repeatedly asking British Cycling performance director Dave Brailsford if it was time to warm-up only to be told to wait for five more minutes. 'I'd like to thank Noel and Liam Gallagher for helping me at that point on my iPod,' said Wiggins, who listened to Oasis' 'Champagne Supernova' in the moments before the final.

Wiggins and McGee had a lot of shared history: McGee had beaten Wiggins to Commonwealth Games gold in Manchester in 2002 and the pair shared a room when they were at the French team Française des Jeux.

Wiggins was the victor on this occasion, and convincingly so, stopping the clock in four minutes 16.304 seconds with McGee almost four seconds behind. 'It's all a bit of a blur at the moment,' Wiggins said. 'This gold medal has been something

LEFT Paul Manning eased Wiggins' passage to Athens by withdrawing from the shortlist for the individual pursuit.

RIGHT Olympic runner-up Brad McGee was magnanimous in defeat in Athens. Also pictured is bronze medallist Sergi Escobar of Spain.

BELOW On the boards on the way to victory in the Athens velodrome.

An Olympic silver medal came in the team pursuit for Wiggins (third left) with Steve Cummings, Paul Manning and Rob Hayles.

I've wanted to do since I was 12 years old, since I watched Chris Boardman win gold in Barcelona. People in cycling want to win yellow jerseys or the Tour de France and I've always dreamed of winning an Olympic gold. This means more to me than anything I'll ever do in my career; I'd be happy if I never win anything ever again.'

Wiggins thanked Brailsford, coach Simon Jones and Boardman for their role in the win. 'This year was all about winning the Olympic gold,' he said. 'It meant quite a disappointing year on the road with my team, Credit Agricole, but that was all part of the sacrifice really, to be in what had to be the form of my life.'

He had been inspired by McGee, who was magnanimous in defeat, saying: 'Congratulations to Bradley. It's a pleasure to race against him. I love that rivalry that two competitors can have on the track and still go down the pub for a beer afterwards.'

A beer had to wait as Wiggins refocused on the team pursuit, but with Jones warning he was far from certain of a place in the final after appearing to be the weakest link in the semi-final of the four-man event. Jones said: 'He was really nervous about riding. He wasn't happy with his performance, he was struggling a bit more than he would have liked.'

Wiggins did feature in the line-up, alongside Hayles, Manning and Steve Cummings, but this time had to settle for silver as favourites Australia, who had won the last two world titles at the expense of their rivals, roared to gold.

'We didn't hold anything back,' Wiggins said. 'But the fact is that we weren't strong enough. The Australian team are the best team pursuit team there has ever been and when there are teams like that there's not a lot you can do.'

Again Wiggins had to refocus, with the Madison alongside Hayles to come. The duo had unfinished business after a late crash ended their medal hopes in Sydney.

'The whole plan when I came here was to win three gold medals,' Wiggins said. 'For the moment I've got a gold and a silver and in the Madison I'll try to rectify what happened four years ago.'

Even before the Madison Wiggins was considering what would happen next, after realising his lifelong ambition. 'I think I'm at a crossroads in my life,' he said. 'The last 12 years of my life I've lived for these few days in August. I told all my teachers at school and they thought I was crazy but I'm 24 now and it's happened. I've never made any plans for my life after this and I've got to sit down for a few months and think about what I want to do now.'

He was determined to enjoy the 200-lap Madison, which can resemble the wacky races and is impossible to predict. There were times when he considered opting out of the event,

before Cath persuaded him otherwise, reminding him of his responsibility to Hayles.

'I'm just going to try to soak it all in because after the individual I was still thinking about the team pursuit,' he said. 'But now it's all over in terms of the pressure events because the Madison is just going to be a bit of fun for us. Already it's a fantastic success for me and if we can go out there and get another medal it'll be a bonus but it's such a lottery of a race. We'll be one of the strongest teams out there and the others will be looking to try and stop us.'

Jones admitted that keeping Wiggins focused ahead of a third event on the schedule was a challenge. 'Bradley is still coming to terms with what he has done,' Jones said. 'He has fulfilled a lifetime's ambition and I can't understand how he feels. It must be an odd feeling, fulfilling a dream. He keeps saying, "This happens to other people, not me." So, hopefully we can get him up for it. We have got a big, big job here and we really want to get a medal in the Madison. We feel they have got the engine for it and it is all about the psychology. We have got a real big job getting Bradley really up for it so he can do his best.'

Just as in Sydney, Hayles crashed, but he and Wiggins had time to recover. Hayles twice had to change bikes and, while his partner was off the track, Wiggins had to keep them in the contest. He did the work of two riders and was required to lap the field to put Britain in medal contention. The pair finished third and the bronze medal meant Wiggins became the first Briton in 40 years to win three medals in a single Games.

'I'm in the form of my life here and I think after the crash I had to stay really calm,' he said. 'It's incredible. It's hard to let it sink in. Growing up in London, I thought this would never happen to me. We're still kind of cocooned in a bit of a bubble in the Olympic Village but it's mind-blowing really.'

Wiggins had escaped from the village for some respite prior to the Madison, meeting fiancée Cath for lunch. 'The individual pursuit was incredible and the team pursuit was hard but we had a day off yesterday and we spent a bit of time away from the village,' Wiggins said. 'I actually had a pint of beer, which did me more good than bad, and we came back today and I was really motivated to win the race.'

Brailsford and Hayles praised Wiggins' success, the best single-Games haul since athlete Mary Rand won in 1964. 'He was born with a natural ability and he has applied himself. He's worked very, very hard,' Brailsford said. 'He's a very driven and focused individual, as most Olympic champions are. He's dreamt of this for 12 years and he's worked to make that dream a reality. Bradley's young. He's got a lot of personality and character and he's an exceptional talent.' Hayles added: 'We knew if we won the Madison he would be the first Briton

'People in cycling want to win yellow jerseys or the Tour de France and I've always dreamed of winning an Olympic gold... I'd be happy if I never win anything ever again.'
– Wiggins on his gold in the individual pursuit

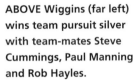

ABOVE Wiggins (far left) wins team pursuit silver with team-mates Steve Cummings, Paul Manning and Rob Hayles.

BELOW Wiggins leads the British quartet across the line during qualifying in Athens, with Chris Newton riding in place of Hayles.

'I'm going to really try and enjoy it and soak it all up. I'm still coming to terms that I'm Olympic champion.'
– Wiggins after Athens

to win two golds in one Games since 1908. But he's got a full set now and hopefully the British public will now take notice of British cycling.'

His achievement had been noticed and rower Matthew Pinsent, who had just won his fourth Olympic gold, approached Wiggins to pass on his congratulations after the Madison. Wiggins later recalled saying to Pinsent: 'What the hell are you doing here?'

Wiggins chose to bask in the glory – and enjoyed more than the occasional pint. Speaking ahead of September's Tour of Britain, he said: 'I'm going to really try and enjoy it and soak it all up. I'm still coming to terms that I'm Olympic champion, it still seems to be something that happens to other people and I don't seem worthy to be in that club yet.

'My race and training programme totally went out of the window after the Olympics and I haven't even had five minutes alone with my partner Cath. I've decided I'll start focusing on my racing again after Christmas, before that I'm going to capitalise on my success and enjoy being an Olympic champion.'

Wiggins featured in an escape on the final stage of the Tour of Britain before taking a break, attending parties, collecting Belgian beer and drinking heavily at his local pub in Derbyshire as he wrestled with what to do next.

Recalling the time, he said: 'I thought I was "it" for a bit after winning those medals, so for a while I was going to parties and enjoying it, but once that started wearing off, I found that I wasn't looking forward to racing my bike. I felt I couldn't be bothered. I just sat around drinking all day. At the time, I thought I was enjoying myself, but I look back and think, what a horrible place to have been.'

The depression was halted, but the drinking was not, as Wiggins and Cath were married on November 5, 2004. Slowly, with Cath expecting, he was coming to terms with the next phase of his life – fatherhood and building on his first Olympic gold.

LEFT As in Sydney, team-mate Rob Hayles crashed in the Madison.

BELOW LEFT Wiggins' efforts while Hayles was off the track ensured a bronze medal.

RIGHT The first British athlete for 40 years to win three medals at a single Games.

BELOW The year ended back on the road – Wiggins (left) climbing Holme Moss, near Holmfirth in the Peak District, on the 2004 Tour of Britain.

A solitary break on stage six of the 2007 Tour de France
earned Wiggins the day's award for most aggressive rider.

ROAD TRIP

4

'I can give the road a few years and will get stronger by riding events like the Tour de France and Tour of Italy.'
– Wiggins prepares for a new focus

ROAD TRIP

After winning Olympic gold in the Athens velodrome, Bradley Wiggins was eager to emulate 1992 champion Chris Boardman and make a successful transition from track to road. 'Everyone wants to see what I can do on the road, me more than anyone else,' he said.

Doping had again plagued road racing, with David Millar, Britain's most recent Tour de France leader, among those serving bans after the Scot admitted using blood booster erythropoietin (EPO). Wiggins followed Boardman's lead. He said: 'If I can adapt for the road that physical potential that I've built up training on a vitamin C tablet from Boots and a multivit, why can't I beat the best in the world on the road on my day? I think Chris took that approach, and Chris was the best in the world on his day. I may be naive, but I think his career spanned the worst time for doping from 1994 to 1998 when he was in his prime.'

Wiggins said his farewell to the velodrome at January's Manchester Track World Cup competition to start his adventure. 'I can give the road a few years and will get stronger by riding events like the Tour de France and Tour of Italy,' he said. 'I can still improve in the pursuit and I'll come back stronger in 2008. I'll be 28, then I'll take it on to London in 2012, when I'll be 32. Maybe I can go on to 2016, although that will be pushing it a bit.'

It was a rare low-key track competition for Wiggins as he missed out on a medal and a new generation began to emerge. Little more than two months later, as a 19-year-old Mark Cavendish won his first Track Cycling World Championships title alongside Rob Hayles in the Madison in Los Angeles in March 2005, Wiggins became a father for the first time with the birth of son Ben, although he missed the crucial moment while travelling back from racing on the Continent.

It was an exciting time, with London bidding for the 2012 Olympic Games and hoping to host the Tour de France's Grand Depart in 2007. 'I'm motivated by winning the Tour de France prologue and perhaps in half a dozen years I may be a contender for the top 10,' Wiggins said. 'I have the physical power, it's just a question of converting it to the road.'

The short-term aim was success in the year's first Grand Tour, the 2005 Giro d'Italia, and his track background meant

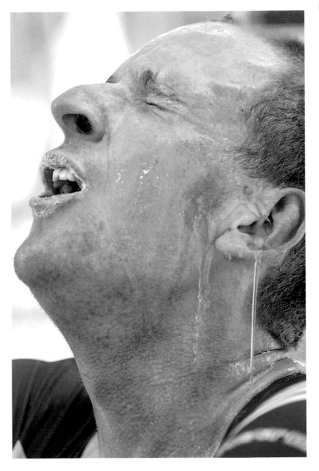

LEFT Heading for a seventh-placed finish in the time-trial at the 2005 road World Championships in Madrid.

ABOVE Showing the strain of competing in the time-trial in the heat of Madrid, where Michael Rogers won a third straight title.

> 'He hasn't made any progress – that's the harsh reality of it. It's [joining Cofidis] not going to help him at all, that's for sure, that I know.'
> – David Millar on Wiggins' Tour de France prospects

he was well-suited for the opening 1.15km prologue in Reggio di Calabria, beside the Strait of Messina. Wiggins finished two seconds behind Brett Lancaster in 11th and rode on to place 123rd of 153 finishers in Milan, more than three and a half hours behind winner Paolo Savoldelli.

After the Tour of Italy, Wiggins considered if the road was really for him, but British Cycling coach Simon Jones insisted he had to find a focus. 'I had a bit of doubt about whether I wanted to continue with the road malarkey, but we decided I had to pick something and hit it with as much effort as I made for the track in Athens,' Wiggins said.

The time-trial at the road World Championships in Madrid in September became his focus and he claimed his most significant road victory to date in the eighth stage of the Tour de l'Avenir, the 'Tour de France of the future', just a few weeks before travelling to Spain. 'I've always targeted two or three things and hit them full-on,' he said. 'Now it's important to find a team who will have confidence in me and let me build a programme for the Tour prologue in Strasbourg next year.'

Wiggins finished seventh in Madrid as Australia's Michael Rogers won for the third successive time, but the future was bright. He signed a two-year deal with Cofidis, with the guarantee of a place in the 2006 Tour de France.

Wiggins opted out of the 2006 Commonwealth Games in Melbourne and Track Cycling World Championships in Bordeaux to focus on the road, but was unhappy with a seventh-placed finish in the Paris-Nice prologue. 'I'm frustrated because I know I am going well and I won't have the chance to use this form again in an event like this for a while,' Wiggins said.

The next opportunity came at the 2006 Dauphiné Liberé, a traditional Tour warm-up, but he trailed in 21st in what he described as the biggest disappointment of his career.

As Millar was preparing to make his return from his two-year suspension, he was asked about Wiggins' prospects in the Tour. 'He hasn't made any progress – that's the harsh reality of it,' Millar said. Millar described Wiggins' Cofidis team, the squad who sacked him following his doping admission, as a 'huge dinosaur'. He said: 'It's not going to help him at all, that's for sure, that I know.'

Final preparations for his first Tour included riding a 10-mile time-trial near Lancaster in a howling gale before he departed for Strasbourg into the midst of the race's biggest doping storm since the Festina affair of 1998.

Ivan Basso, Jan Ullrich and Francisco Mancebo were implicated in the Operacion Puerto doping ring and were denied the right to start the race; the trio had been among the favourites to succeed retired seven-time winner Lance Armstrong as champion. Wiggins said: 'It's about time they got rid of these sods if they are proven to be doing stuff. Guys like me have to endure them making our lives hard in the mountains and what happened is brilliant from that point of view.'

The 7.1km prologue was won by Thor Hushovd, with Wiggins four seconds behind in 16th place, one place ahead of Millar. It was a satisfactory result, but he was determined to make an impression, and on the fourth stage to Saint-Quentin he was part of the day's five-man escape, only to be swept up shortly before the finish.

'I've shown I'm part of the event and on a day like today you never know,' he said. 'If we had not been riding into a headwind we might have stayed away to the finish. It's my role to do this sort of thing until we get to the mountains and it was a couple of hours for Cofidis on live television.'

The mountain stages saw Wiggins fall from the front of the race into the *grupetto*. As he suffered as a back-marker, Wiggins was not aware of the remarkable events which were unfolding ahead of him. Floyd Landis, the yellow jersey incumbent, struggled so terribly on the 16th stage to La

RIGHT Wiggins was now a Cofidis rider, but the partnership was to end disastrously.

'This race is so **** hard that I can't envisage doing it next year.'**
– Wiggins on his first Tour de France

Toussuire that he finished 10 minutes behind and plummeted to 11th place overall. A day later the American resurrected his hopes at the Col de Joux-Plane in Morzine, rising to within 30 seconds of the lead, as Wiggins toiled along, finishing more than 52 minutes behind. The experience left him broken and uncertain whether the Tour really was for him, even with the prospect of a London prologue 11 months away. 'This race is so bloody hard that I can't envisage doing it next year,' Wiggins said. 'I don't feel any excitement about it. This was my childhood dream, like being Olympic champion was. I'd love to win a stage of the Tour, but unless I win on the Champs-Elysees, I'd need to come back and at the moment, if I never ride it again, I'd be happy.'

It was perhaps fatigue speaking, as he placed 124th of 139 finishers, three hours 25 minutes behind Landis. His mood soured further when four days later, while travelling to Chester Zoo with wife Cath and Ben, the news broke that Landis had tested positive for testosterone. 'It was one of the best Tours for many years, to be part of it made me proud, but a few days afterwards the whole thing evaporated,' Wiggins said.

Again he questioned whether the Tour was right for him and if his love for road racing had disappeared, but Shane Sutton was adamant Wiggins could improve and the birth of his daughter, Isabella, provided perspective. 'I came out of the Tour a bit of a wreck, and confidence was at a low,' Wiggins said. 'I'd not really done anything I could point to and say "yeah, I'm happy with that", but Shane worked on me, started talking to me about what was coming up and gradually I started to feel better.'

Wiggins was wounded further ahead of the February 2007 Manchester Track World Cup meeting when a towel he was using while training on static rollers became caught in his front wheel. He was thrown over the handlebars as the wheel locked, suffering a groin strain and a cut above his eye which required eight stitches. Wiggins recovered and won the team

ABOVE A return to the track brought Wiggins (far right) victory in the team pursuit at the 2007 track World Championships in Majorca, alongside Geraint Thomas, Ed Clancy and Paul Manning.

OPPOSITE The individual pursuit world title was added to the team version in Majorca.

RIGHT Celebrating his individual pursuit success with baby daughter Isabella, while son Ben shows an early allegiance to Wigan rugby league club.

The 2007 Dauphiné Liberé saw Wiggins don a yellow
jersey for the first time in his road career.

'It was 3am on a Sunday – most people were too drunk to notice me. There weren't any cars about and I did break a few traffic laws, but it was an exception.'
– Wiggins on his unorthodox preparations for the London prologue to the 2007 Tour de France

pursuit and individual pursuit to prove his ability on the boards remained; his individual win came in the fastest time since the Olympics. 'I love the track but I just needed a break after Athens,' he said. 'It was quite an emotional time for me, becoming an Olympic champion, but I've grown up a lot since then. I did the Tour which was a dream and it makes stuff like this seem quite easy. The Tour puts things into perspective as to what's hard.'

Wiggins won individual pursuit and team pursuit gold medals at the Track Cycling World Championships in Palma, Majorca in March before road duty resumed. The fallout of the Landis affair was continuing, but Wiggins expressed faith in the testing procedures and talked up his Cofidis team's change in mentality and approach. 'They have come out the other end of the tunnel and they really want to portray the new image of young, clean, French and foreign riders,' he said.

Wiggins knew he was yet to fulfil his potential and was targeting London as the 2007 Tour visited the capital for the first time. He entered the race in fine form after scoring prologue victories in the Four Days of Dunkirk and the Dauphiné Liberé, where he secured a first yellow jersey.

'I'm in my sixth year as a pro and I only got my third win on the road,' he said. 'When I turned pro, everyone knew I had the potential for doing things like this. Now I believe this win gives me the status of a favourite for the prologue of the Tour de France, which I wasn't before.'

Wiggins rode the 7.9km central London route, just a few miles from where he grew up, in the dark in preparation. He said: 'It was 3am on a Sunday – most people were too drunk to notice me. I wanted to get a real feel for the course and take some of the corners at high speed. It is the only way in London you can really cycle on it because parts of the course are one-way. There weren't any cars about and I did break a few traffic laws, but it was an exception.'

More than a million people stood by the roadside as Swiss ace Fabian Cancellara won, with Wiggins far from disconsolate

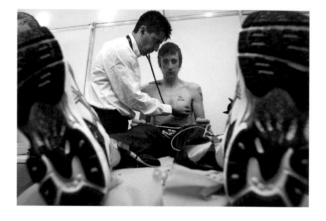

ABOVE Undergoing a medical examination before the 2007 Tour de France.

OPPOSITE Passing the Houses of Parliament on his way to fourth place in the 2007 prologue.

BELOW On the Cofidis bus before it all went sour for the French team.

in fourth. 'I never expected this magnitude of people so God knows what the Olympics will be like,' he said. 'This is how the Tour de France should be, not like last year.'

Wiggins completed the first week on the attack on a day-long solo escape to Bourg-en-Bresse on the 40th anniversary of the death of Tom Simpson, Britain's first Tour leader. Although Wiggins knew his solo effort would be doomed when the sprinters' teams set to work, he had an altogether different reason for his move on the sixth stage. 'It was my wife Cath's birthday, I knew she'd be watching with the kids, so it was a good way to spend the day with them,' said Wiggins, who was awarded a place on the Tour podium for the first time as the day's most aggressive rider. On the same day, British Cycling performance director Dave Brailsford made public his vision of a British road team for the first time.

While there appeared to be hope for the future, the past was all too present for Wiggins. Alexandre Vinokourov tested positive for an illegal blood transfusion and his Astana team were expelled from the race after the Kazakh had won the stage 13 time-trial in Albi and the 15th stage. 'It is a disaster for the sport. There will be no cycling in 10 years if this goes on,' Wiggins said.

But worse was to follow as race leader Michael Rasmussen was fired by his Rabobank team for lying about his whereabouts leading up to the Tour. It left the peloton without a rider in the yellow jersey on the 17th stage from Pau to Castelsarrasin, with Alberto Contador the new race leader.

Wiggins did not start the 17th stage after becoming unwittingly embroiled in the next Tour scandal. He had finished almost 42 minutes behind as Rasmussen won the 16th stage to the summit of the Col d'Aubisque, falling almost three and a half hours behind overall. On his arrival at the finish, Wiggins was informed that his Cofidis team leader Cristian Moreni, who was almost two hours off the pace in 54th overall, had tested positive for testosterone and the team exited the race, with Wiggins disgusted. He was taken in for

police questioning and flew home the following day after borrowing a top from Millar, now a friend, with his Cofidis kit discarded in a bin at Pau airport. 'It is completely gutting to have to quit the Tour,' Wiggins said. 'It makes you think about your future as a professional cyclist. You say to yourself "what is the point? I could be doing better things".'

On his return home, Wiggins held a media conference in the familiar, safe confines of the Manchester Velodrome. 'My initial reaction was "I'm going to get out of the sport",' he said. 'But then you think why not continue because I get a lot of pleasure out of it. Why should I give up because of one individual? So far on this Tour five people have spoiled it out of nearly 200 who started in London. The start in London was amazing but things slowly started deteriorating. It's not a nice place to be. No-one has got any faith in who is yellow now. I think the whole thing is now null and void as far as this year is concerned.'

He remained bullish, though, adding: 'It has made me determined to come through this whole thing and prove that there can be clean winners in this sport. That made my determination even stronger.'

Wiggins returned to the track, riding in the Ghent Six-Day race with Cavendish and at the Track World Cup meetings in Sydney and Beijing, the latter meeting doubling as the test event for the following summer's Olympic Games. The test went well for Wiggins, who cruised to victory in a time well adrift of his best in an indication he would be the man to beat in China.

FINE CHINA

Bradley Wiggins leads Ed Clancy, Paul Manning and Geraint Thomas to gold in the team pursuit in Beijing in 2008.

'The big aim is always the Olympics but we've prepared well for this. I do believe we can go faster.'

– Wiggins before the 2008 Olympics

FINE CHINA

The Cofidis saga frustrated Bradley Wiggins and the track became his full focus ahead of a third Olympics. August's 2008 Games in Beijing were on his mind a lot, but his attention was diverted after being awoken from a deep sleep by a telephone call in the early hours of one January morning in 2008.

Shane Sutton, Wiggins' mentor and something of a father figure, called after hearing from contacts in Australia that Wiggins' father, Gary, had been hospitalised. The 55-year-old Gary Wiggins was soon confirmed dead after being discovered unconscious in a street in the town of Aberdeen in the Hunter Valley, north of Sydney, early one Friday morning. Police suspected he was either beaten or fell over while drunk, with a post-mortem examination finding he died from an injury to the head.

Wiggins was shocked and saddened at the death, but had long cut his father from his life; Gary had not met his wife Cath, or their two children, Ben and Isabella. As with the passing of any relation, there was a period of reflection, considering what might have been, pondering the short reconciliations which usually ended as a result of Gary's dysfunctional ways; the deepest thoughts coming as Wiggins rode through the Lancashire drizzle, enhancing his endurance for his track challenge.

Wiggins did not dwell for long. The familiar surroundings of the Manchester Velodrome were to hold the 2008 Track Cycling World Championships in March, with hosts Britain seeking to continue to show their supremacy after a strong showing in Palma the previous year and, as an Olympic gold medallist from Athens, Wiggins was one of the team totems.

It was a difficult opening day of the World Championships for the hosts as Rob Hayles, with whom Wiggins won Madison bronze in Athens, was withdrawn after being found to have a haematocrit reading above the permitted levels. It was not

LEFT Madison victory with Mark Cavendish in the 2008 Track World Championships was not a sign of things to come.

RIGHT The individual pursuit brought one of three world champion's rainbow jerseys on the home track in Manchester.

58

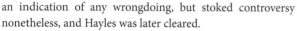

'People will jump to the worst-case scenario but Rob is one of the longest-serving guys on this programme and one of the cleanest guys around.'
– Wiggins on Rob Hayles' withdrawal from the World Championships

an indication of any wrongdoing, but stoked controversy nonetheless, and Hayles was later cleared.

There was another surprise when Wiggins, the reigning Olympic champion and defending world champion, finished behind Holland's Jenning Huizenga in qualifying for the individual pursuit. He soon responded, winning gold by almost five seconds before providing Hayles with his backing. 'People will jump to the worst-case scenario but Rob is one of the longest-serving guys on this programme and one of the cleanest guys around,' Wiggins said.

A day later Wiggins demonstrated his form in a team pursuit victory which augured well for China. He combined with Ed Clancy, Geraint Thomas and Paul Manning to set a world record of three minutes 56.322 seconds, beating Australia's Olympic-winning mark from four years earlier. Wiggins said: 'The big aim is always the Olympics but we've prepared well for this. I do believe we can go faster.'

Wiggins had more to give and made it a golden treble with victory alongside Mark Cavendish in the Madison, heightening expectations that in Beijing he could add to his gold, silver and bronze haul from Athens with a golden clean sweep. While the pursuit events appeared controllable and within his grasp, the Madison was difficult to predict. The tandem event, where team-mates sling-shot each other into the race, is fraught with danger over 200 laps, with spectacular crashes frequent and favourites often marked out of the race.

'The Madison is so unpredictable – this just means it's going to be even harder for the Olympics,' said Wiggins, after donning a third rainbow jersey of the week.

Wiggins and Cavendish were again team-mates in May's Giro d'Italia, riding for Team Columbia, and Wiggins was part

RIGHT Leading Ed Clancy, Geraint Thomas and Paul Manning to victory in the team pursuit at the 2008 Track World Championships in Manchester.

FINE CHINA

> 'He's got a pretty heavy programme. I don't want him to go for the record, I just want him to win three golds.'
> – Coach Shane Sutton on Wiggins' Olympic programme

of the squad which helped Cavendish to his first two Grand Tour stage wins, in Catanzaro Lungomare and Cittadella, before placing fourth in the concluding time-trial in Milan.

As Wiggins returned to the track to hone his Olympic preparations at the British team's training camp in Newport, Cavendish took to the road and again demonstrated his supreme talent by winning four stages of the Tour de France.

Rather than ride on to Paris, Cavendish withdrew from the Tour early to focus on his first Olympics in Beijing. Wiggins talked up his Madison colleague's ability ahead of the duo's quest for Games glory. 'Cav's performances were no surprise,' he said. 'If he had stayed to the end in Paris, he would have won five stages. He has come out at the right time, and he has got the best part of four weeks to get himself right. He will be ready to go, definitely.'

British Cycling performance director Dave Brailsford had thought of every detail and at their base in south Wales: his charges were even shown how to wash their hands by a surgeon, in order to reduce the risk of picking up any illness.

Wiggins was in such strong form that in training he bettered Chris Boardman's individual pursuit world record of four minutes 11.114 seconds, which had been set in the aerodynamic 'Superman' position, with arms outstretched, which was later outlawed. But the following day he fell ill – perhaps after failing to wash his hands properly after one too many handshakes at the media day. A period of enforced rest ensured a speedy recovery and despite a few days off the bike, Wiggins proved his fitness with a strong training performance before departing for the airport.

Britain's cyclists travelled to China backed to bring home the bounty after Palma and Manchester, and the track team were buoyed by Nicole Cooke's road race win by the Great Wall of China. Wiggins had recovered and was thriving, proving his condition at the Laoshan Velodrome by qualifying fastest in the individual pursuit as he sought to defend his title. He appeared comfortable in reducing the Olympic record he set

four years earlier in Athens, but talk of beating Boardman's best was downplayed. Sutton said: 'He's got a pretty heavy programme. I don't want him to go for the record, I just want him to win three golds.'

Wiggins duly delivered the first, finishing ahead of New Zealand's Hayden Roulston in the final, five seconds behind the world record but with energy to spare. Steven Burke was third after taking the second pursuit place ahead of Cavendish. 'In the final, I just had a job to do – there was no chasing world records,' Wiggins said. 'I'm racing tomorrow morning with the boys and this is just phase one of three.'

Wiggins was aiming to make the most of his talents with his three-event target, having learned the lessons of 2004. 'Athens nearly destroyed me and I paid the consequences of that afterwards,' he said. 'I was quite a mature athlete but an immature person. To come out and beat Brad McGee in the Olympic final was just something that I'd worked myself up to all year. I was in such a kind of pent-up emotional state once it was over that was it, it had taken so much out of me mentally. I underperformed in the team pursuit final – couldn't give a monkey's about it, basically – then the next day I had a day off and I just wanted to go home. I'd had enough really. I didn't want to get up in the Olympic arena again... The Madison was just a case of, "Okay, I'll get up and enjoy it". We were the strongest team on the track but we came away with a bronze. Then afterwards I had months off the bike and lived it up.'

Wiggins had worked with British Cycling psychiatrist Steve Peters to control his emotions, or his 'inner chimp', as the doctor described it. 'I don't do emotion any more,' Wiggins said. 'I've worked with Steve Peters on that closely the last 12 months. I've got to the stage where I now enjoy my sport and don't get so hyped up.' Wiggins was determined to deliver in the

RIGHT Gold medal number one in Beijing came when Wiggins successfully defended his Olympic individual pursuit title.

ABOVE The Olympic individual pursuit gold medal lies on the dais as a phone call is made after the presentation ceremony.

RIGHT AND LEFT Muscles are tuned on a static bike in the Laoshan Velodrome in Beijing.

four-man team pursuit and the British squad took the event to new heights. In a scintillating performance, the quartet annihilated the opposition, Denmark finishing a distant second as Wiggins, Clancy, Thomas and Manning lowered their own world record to three minutes 53.314 seconds, 48 hours and three rides after Wiggins had won the individual title. 'The individual was quite surreal – I enjoyed it for about half an hour and then the medal went in the drawer and I was thinking if we didn't win tonight, what a huge disappointment this would be,' he said.

'It's just fantastic to be part of this team. We've come a long way in four years and to put a time like that on the board is phenomenal. I'm just delighted.'

Wiggins was required to race for a fifth straight day in the Madison, seeking a fourth Olympic gold and a third at a single Games. Chris Hoy, having won the team sprint and keirin, was also seeking to emulate swimmer Henry Taylor as the first Briton to win three golds in a single Games for 100 years and was set to ride in the latter stages of the sprint.

'Any medal won't do tomorrow, it's got to be gold,' Wiggins said. 'But the Madison is the hardest of the lot – anything can happen. You can be the strongest of the lot and have a crash early so we'll see.'

For Wiggins, who it was later revealed had again been struggling with illness, it was a race too far. The British pair, with Cavendish attempting to spark Wiggins for one last effort, finished a lowly ninth as Argentina won the Olympic title. It left Cavendish distraught and suffering the ignominy of being the only member of Britain's track team to leave the Laoshan Velodrome without a medal.

The duo left the arena without commenting, with Brailsford saying: 'The harsh reality of it was that Brad was tired from all the events he had already done and today that showed. They're both great, great riders and today wasn't their day. A different day, a different race and things work out differently.'

The fallout lasted for some time after the event. In September, Wiggins revealed he and Cavendish were yet to be reconciled. 'Cav is like my little brother and I love him dearly, but we left the stadium without saying a word to each other and we've yet to speak,' he said. 'I was knackered but he was bit cocky. Who wouldn't be when you're 22, you've just won four stages of the Tour de France and you're riding with a double Olympic champion?'

Wiggins failed to appear at a media conference at the end of the track cycling programme, when Hoy was the centre of

'Cav is like my little brother and I love him dearly, but we left the stadium without saying a word to each other.'
– Wiggins on the Madison disappointment

LEFT The Madison world title with Mark Cavendish could not be converted into Olympic gold as the British pair finished ninth.

ABOVE A second successive Olympic individual pursuit title confirmed Wiggins' dominance over 4km.

BELOW Team pursuit gold followed at the Beijing Games with, from left, Paul Manning, Ed Clancy, Geraint Thomas.

LEFT Cath Wiggins (centre) celebrates as her husband wins another Olympic gold medal in the team pursuit in Beijing.

attention after bagging three golds as part of a British haul of seven gold medals from 10 events. 'He was disappointed but he doesn't deserve to go home a disappointed man,' Brailsford said of Wiggins. 'I guess each performance needs to be seen in isolation. Actually, if they'd been the only two gold medals we'd won at the Olympic Games, seen in isolation, they'd be incredible.'

Wiggins attracted further attention, this time from the Chinese police, after provoking the ire of a taxi driver by rolling over the bonnet of his parked car. He had been celebrating his two gold medals at London House, the venue in Beijing set up to promote the British capital ahead of the 2012 Games, and the intervention of the police was required to calm the situation. Wiggins' charm also helped, plus the input of Steve Cram, the BBC athletics commentator. 'It ended up very good-natured with photos being taken of him, the driver and his medals,' a British Olympic Association spokeswoman reported.

A few hours later, Wiggins checked in for his flight home and was upgraded to first class in recognition of his success; Cavendish was stranded in economy. Cavendish had borrowed a medal from a team-mate, but an air stewardess recognised him and denied him access to the first-class cabin, where only gold and silver medal winners were welcome.

Wiggins returned home to Lancashire to ponder the future. He joined calls for Hoy to be knighted and his ears would have pricked up when hearing Brailsford's future plans – to launch a British team and win the Tour. Like Wiggins, Brailsford was seeking a new challenge. Brailsford said: 'What's going to get me out of bed in the morning, really put a smile on my face and think, "Wow, I can't believe I've got the chance to do this today"? It'd be bike racing, that's what pushes my buttons. If somebody said to me "what's your dream job?" that's what I'd want to do. If I was a multi-millionaire and could do anything, I'd try to win the Tour de France.'

Sky had announced a sponsorship deal with British Cycling prior to the Olympics and people began to put two and two

together. Wiggins was eager for a British professional team to be launched, believing the critical mass of talent – himself, Cavendish, Thomas and others – was available to make it a success.

Wiggins said: 'They are in the early stages of putting that together and it would be phenomenal. We have got the talent so it is definitely likely now. You need the right team and a sponsor who is going to put up £8million a year and they appear to have that. I don't know who it is yet but Sky have come on board and made a big commitment. And if a company like Sky gets involved with British cycling then a lot of others will as well.

'We already have the back-up team with Dave Brailsford, who has put this whole thing together for British cycling, and Shane Sutton. Then, of course, you need the riders and there are enough of us out there.'

Wiggins was also eyeing an opportunity to emulate Cavendish's road successes at the Tour. 'I just want to win a stage,' he said. 'I came close last year when I had a third and a fourth. I have been within a couple of kilometres of winning a stage so it is definitely achievable. I have the ability to do it, it is just that it is so different to the track. I use the analogy that it is like Seb Coe taking on the marathon. He definitely had the engine for it as an Olympic champion on the track but to make that step up would take some doing.'

Wiggins rode in the Tour of Britain in September and returned to the velodrome in November as Britain celebrated their Olympic achievement in the Track World Cup event at the Manchester Velodrome.

But a year which began with the death of his father and featured three world titles and two Olympic gold medals dwindled to a conclusion as he finished the weekend without a medal, his Madison partnership with Thomas failing to flourish. Hoy finished the year as BBC Sports Personality of the Year and, while Wiggins certainly did not begrudge his team-mate's success, he knew he was capable of more.

ABOVE Showing off gold medals with Chris Hoy, who was to become the first British athlete for 100 years to win three golds at a single Games.

LEFT Wiggins had to settle for two golds at the Beijing Olympics, but he was made a CBE when the 2009 New Year Honours were announced.

'He was disappointed but he doesn't deserve to go home a disappointed man. If they'd been the only two gold medals we'd won at the Olympic Games, seen in isolation, they'd be incredible.'
– Performance director Dave Brailsford

A DAWN SKY

Bradley Wiggins' much-anticipated move to the new Team Sky was finally announced in December 2009.

stage to Mont Ventoux, the unforgiving giant of Provence with its lunar landscape, where Tom Simpson died 42 years earlier after collapsing exhausted and was later found to have taken a cocktail of drugs. Wiggins, a student of the sport, paid homage, carrying a photograph of Simpson as he sealed fourth overall, behind Contador, to equal the best Tour result by a British rider, set by Robert Millar 25 years earlier.

The following day, Cavendish won his sixth stage of the race in Paris, capping a hugely successful Tour for Britain; four years earlier 'Les Rosbifs' did not have a rider in the race.

Wiggins said: 'To finish fourth changes everything. The Olympics are fantastic for the two weeks they're on every four years, but the Tour de France is where it's at. I'd like to win Olympic gold and win the Tour in the same year. My success this year has fed my hunger.'

With Team Sky set to launch the following season, speculation mounted of a Wiggins move. It was a natural fit, but Wiggins was under contract with Garmin until the end of 2010. Reports continually surfaced saying a deal was near, with one stating Brailsford had travelled to New York to broker a deal, when in fact he was at the Manchester Velodrome overseeing the track squad.

Wiggins, speaking to the BBC in Mendrisio, Switzerland ahead of the road 2009 World Championships, revealed his thoughts on the matter. 'To win the Champions League you go to Man United and I'm probably playing at Wigan at the moment,' Wiggins said. He later attempted to downplay his comments, while Garmin manager Jonathan Vaughters proclaimed: 'I'd have to be clinically insane to sell the contract.'

On Wednesday, December 9, 2009, Team Sky called a media conference for the following day in central London. Vaughters had relented and the worst-kept secret in cycling was set to be revealed. On a pivotal day for the sport, when the International Olympic Committee confirmed changes to the London 2012 track programme which included the removal of the individual pursuit, Wiggins joined Team Sky. The four-year deal was announced yards from the Cumberland Hotel where he used to cut carrots and mop the floors as a kitchen hand during his teenage years.

'There was only one team I would have left for and that was to come home to Sky and to Dave,' he said. 'There was no way I couldn't be involved with this from the start.'

Vaughters agreed to a 'settlement', but was frustrated. 'Fourteen months ago, there was only one team knocking on Brad's door and that was me,' Vaughters said. 'I liked his talent and it was something I recognised a long time ago when everyone else was thinking of him as a track rider.' David Millar, a team-mate at Garmin, was annoyed too. 'The reason he got fourth last year was because of us,' said Millar, who

RIGHT Wiggins remembered Tom Simpson's tragic death 42 years earlier on the fearsome climb up Mont Ventoux.

'It's not great, but what can I do? Go home or stay here and battle for the next two weeks and see what happens.'
– Wiggins on his Tour de France struggles

warned Wiggins might struggle as Team Sky figurehead. 'He's not a natural leader.' Wiggins made a winning start to life at Team Sky, with victory in the Tour of Qatar's team time-trial, and then opened the British squad's Grand Tour campaign with a bang. He won the opening prologue of the 2010 Giro d'Italia in Amsterdam, becoming the second Briton to don the leader's *maglia rosa*, but a gruelling race would take its toll as his attentions turned from pink to yellow.

Wiggins set the time record for ascending the Rocacorba climb near Girona, Spain, a fitness test he used with Garmin in 2009, before travelling to the Tour. He described his condition as 'as good as it gets' ahead of the prologue in Rotterdam, but behind the words, there was a lingering doubt.

Then Brailsford, renowned for analysing every detail, went against convention in the prologue, sending Wiggins down the ramp earlier than his overall rivals, believing he would benefit from better weather – data from Britain's Olympic sailing team had been used to forecast conditions – and increased recovery time.

The rain arrived earlier than anticipated. As he was warming-up inside the mechanic's truck to avoid the attention of onlookers, Wiggins was told 'don't do a Boardman'. It was a reference to three-times prologue winner Boardman crashing out of the 1995 Tour just a few minutes into the prologue.

Overburdened by leadership, expectation and concern over the damp road surface, Wiggins finished a lowly 77th behind winner Fabian Cancellara. He was adamant the 56 seconds lost would prove insignificant, but it provided a worrying indication.

As soon as the race went uphill, Wiggins faded. Armstrong admitted defeat after a woeful eighth stage to Morzine-Avoriaz and Wiggins might have done so as well. On the first rest day in a cellar bar in the French ski resort, Wiggins revealed concern. He said: 'It's not great, but what can I do? Go home or stay here and battle for the next two weeks and see what happens.' The following day Wiggins fell further adrift and further

torment came in the Pyrenees. In Ax-3-Domaines, with six days of racing remaining, he cracked after falling more than 11 minutes behind leader Andy Schleck. 'I just feel consistently mediocre,' he said. 'Last year was a bit of a fluke, in the sense that it wasn't planned throughout the year. I fell into superb form and was riding on cloud nine most of the race. I haven't lived up to my expectation.'

As Contador and Andy Schleck duelled for the yellow jersey up the mist-shrouded Col du Tourmalet, Team Sky and Wiggins began a period of introspection. 'It's always the first climb of the Tour when you realise that you've got it or you haven't,' he said. 'Last year that was Andorra and I was right there with them; this year it was Morzine and I wasn't. We'll take a lot away from it, make some changes and come back next year stronger.'

For the second successive year Wiggins finished one place behind Armstrong, only this time it was in 24th place, upgraded to 23rd when Contador was later stripped of the title and banned for a doping offence.

It was a miserable Tour for Wiggins, whose grandfather, his substitute father, died during the race.

The music fan compared the Tour to 'second album syndrome' and retained the belief that a 'platinum album' remained within. 'Sometimes you have to fail at something to realise how to do it,' he said.

Shane Sutton introduced Wiggins to Tim Kerrison, a sports scientist with a background in swimming and rowing. Kerrison recognised the flaws in performance – suffering in the heat, at altitude and on the climbs – and worked on a strategy to deliver Tour success.

Wiggins bought into the plan, using his garden shed as a heat chamber, while keeping his Olympic options open.

He returned to the velodrome, winning the team pursuit at the Manchester Track World Cup in February 2011, before finishing third overall in the Paris-Nice stage race. Team Sky were no longer all about one rider and one race and Wiggins

RIGHT Victory in the Critérium du Dauphiné fed growing optimisim about Wiggins' chances in the Tour de France.

BELOW Awaiting the presentation ceremony at the British road race championship, surrounded by Dave Brailsford and children Ben and Isabella.

OPPOSITE The 2011 Tour de France ended with the road cyclist's all-too-familiar broken collarbone.

was thriving. He claimed the most prestigious triumph of his road career to date, in the traditional Tour warm-up, the Critérium du Dauphiné, before winning the British road race title in Northumberland.

The Team Sky bus was parked on the village green in Stamfordham, with Cavendish an onboard guest which fanned further speculation that he was about to switch to the British squad. A deal was still to be done, but the effervescent Cavendish was busy choosing his bus seat for the following season, with Wiggins, who had moved from the back to sit at the front as leader, joking with Brailsford as to whether signing Cavendish would be a good idea.

Wiggins travelled to the 2011 Tour's start in the Vendee, western France, seeking to 'get back to the heights of 2009' and Team Sky enjoyed their first Tour stage win when Edvald Boasson Hagen took the sixth stage. Wiggins was only 10 seconds behind in sixth place but jubilation turned to despair on stage seven as he fractured a collarbone on the road to Chateauroux.

Through painkillers, Wiggins was philosophical, famously telling ITV4: 'It's unfortunate but life goes on. I've got fantastic form and it's only a broken collarbone. I'll recover from it and be back. I feel top of the world now, I had some fantastic drugs.'

Wiggins had a plate inserted into his shoulder and the Vuelta a Espana, which was set to begin on August 20, and the World Championships time-trial quickly became targets as he looked ahead to a Tour and Olympic double in 2012.

Wiggins was advised to not watch the Tour, but he was able to detach himself from the race and enjoy Cadel Evans' triumph. 'I found it inspirational watching it at home,' Wiggins said. 'He gave hope to a lot of people out there, the way he won it and the manner in which he won it, and it certainly inspired me to try to do it myself.'

Benidorm, the starting point for the Vuelta, marked the beginning of Wiggins' adventure. In an eventful race, Wiggins

**'Next year is going to be very exciting.
I believe now more than ever that I am
capable of winning the Tour.'**
– Wiggins ends 2011 in optimistic mood

and team-mate Chris Froome each wore the leader's red jersey before Juan Jose Cobo overtook the duo on the fearsome Alto de L'Angliru climb. It was a decisive move and Froome and Wiggins had to settle for second and third place respectively, in a landmark moment – it was the first time two Britons had stood together on the podium at a Grand Tour. Wiggins said: 'With my shoulder as it was this race was always going to be a bit of a testing ground for me and I'm really happy. This race has proved that what happened two years ago at the Tour de France was no fluke and I know in my mind now that I have what it takes to match strong riders at the Tour next year.'

His focus turned to the 2011 road World Championships in Copenhagen, where he finished second to Tony Martin of Germany in the time-trial. Wiggins was then part of the team effort which set up a sprint for Cavendish to become the first British men's road race world champion since Simpson in 1965. Strong bonds were formed – there was a reconciliation with Millar and the performance was key to Cavendish agreeing a move to Team Sky the following month.

For Wiggins, the journey from Chateauroux to Copenhagen was an eventful one, but heightened his belief of further success in 2012. 'The whole year really has been fantastic progress for me,' he said. 'Next year is going to be very exciting. I believe now more than ever that I am capable of winning the Tour.'

ABOVE Wiggins' World Championships time-trial efforts were rewarded only with second place behind Tony Martin.

RIGHT The 2011 Vuelta a Espana offered a hint of the future as Wiggins (left) and Chris Froome flanked winner Juan Jose Cobo on the podium.

FAR RIGHT Time-trial disappointment in Copenhagen was put aside as Wiggins (in Union Jack helmet) helped Mark Cavendish to the road race world title.

TOUR TRIUMPH

Bradley Wiggins wears the leader's yellow jersey as the peloton rolls through classic Tour de France scenery.

'Paris is a long way off. We saw that last year. I was in hospital after seven days.'
– Wiggins on the eve of the 2012 Tour

of time-trials, riding alone against the clock, were going to be just as important.

Wiggins was unfazed by being labelled a favourite when faced with the world's media at his Belgian hotel on the eve of the 6.4-kilometre Liège prologue. He had rarely experienced attention like it, other than when his team-mate Cristian Moreni was thrown off the 2007 Tour. Cavendish was used to such focus, but the Manxman had to take second billing.

'It's the stuff of dreams for me, being a fan of the sport,' Wiggins said. 'I'd never imagined that one day I'll be favourite for the Tour. Kids from Kilburn didn't become favourites for the Tour – you were either a postman, a milkman or worked in the Ladbrokes. We're in a brilliant position and I think it's something to be celebrated.'

Wiggins knew though that being labelled a favourite and his words, published on websites and printed in newspapers across the globe, meant little, particularly after his experience 12 months earlier in Chateauroux.

He said: 'Paris is a long way off. We saw that last year. I was in hospital after seven days. The next three weeks are going to decide this Tour and not what you say.'

Unlike in Rotterdam, Wiggins planned to go flat out and race from the start, just like in any other bike race. As Team Sky leader, Wiggins was among the last of the 198-man peloton to roll down the start ramp and little more than seven minutes later his day's racing was complete, in second place, seven seconds behind Fabian Cancellara. The distance was minute in the context of the 3,497km race to Paris, but the performance showed Wiggins was peaking at the right time. 'I did say to the team last night there was one man who could beat me and that was always Fabian – he's the king of those things,' Wiggins said. 'It's the perfect start.'

The first real test came on the first road stage, which finished with a climb to Seraing. The pace was frenetic by the banks of the Meuse river as the entire peloton fought for position approaching the finishing ascent and Wiggins benefited from

a stroke of good fortune. He rolled over a hole in the road and was immediately followed by team-mate Chris Froome, who suffered a puncture and lost over a minute as a result. Had Wiggins suffered the flat tyre, he would have had a major deficit to overcome. There were numerous moments in a frantic and crash-strewn first week which reminded Wiggins how perilous his position was, not least the loss of team-mate Kanstantsin Siutsou who crashed and sustained a broken leg. David Millar, riding in his 11th Tour, described it as 'the scariest crash I've ever been in' on stage six to Metz. Cavendish narrowly avoided the carnage, but was stranded with a flat tyre as team-mates stayed with Wiggins, leaving the Manxman cast adrift and sacrificing a potential sprint stage win to support their leader. It provided a full indication

Le TOUR
de FRANCE
2012

ABOVE Preparing to roll
off the starting ramp with
3,497km to go until Paris.

LEFT The centre of
attention even during
last-minute preparations
in Liège.

of Team Sky's strategy and the focus on Wiggins, without compromise, and came a day after the squad had heeded the instruction from team principal Dave Brailsford to 'stop dithering' in the middle of a nervous peloton during the first week. In Metz, Brailsford said: 'The first phase of this race is now over and he's still upright on his bike, which was the main objective, and he hasn't lost any time.'

The second phase saw Team Sky, Wiggins and Froome show their strength at La Planche des Belles Filles, the first summit finish of the Tour on stage seven. Cancellara knew his hold on the *maillot jaune* was set to come to an end and Wiggins' squad were the day's dominant force, riding at a high tempo which decimated the field. Edvald Boasson Hagen and Christian Knees led the peloton on the lower ramps, with Porte and Michael Rogers taking over as the gradient increased. The Team Sky strategy was supremely executed. Froome accelerated to the line to take the victory, with Wiggins content to follow the wheel of defending champion Cadel Evans and claim third place and the yellow jersey for the first time. 'To be here, on the top of a mountain in the yellow jersey is phenomenal,' Wiggins said. 'This was the plan; it's what we've trained for all year, but until you go through the process and put it into action and do like we did today... it's an incredible feeling.' Wiggins was acutely aware of the significance of becoming the

fifth Briton to don the *maillot jaune*, but with the jersey comes additional responsibility – the daily focus and scrutiny of the world's media for one.

Wiggins survived Evans' attempt to eat into his deficit on the road to Porrentruy as the Tour made a brief sojourn to Switzerland on stage eight before an emotional and expletive-laden outburst on the topic of doping, a subject all Tour leaders are asked to address, given the history of the sport.

Wiggins was asked about Team Sky's performance on stage seven – a dominant display provoked some commentators, particularly on Twitter, to compare the British squad's performance with that of seven-times winner Lance Armstrong's United States Postal Service squad in their heyday – and the cynics who suggest riders have to take drugs to win the Tour. Armstrong has always denied doping, but the inference of the question was plain, as was Wiggins' response:

'I say they're just ******* *******. I cannot be doing with people like that,' Wiggins said. 'It justifies their own bone-

BELOW Chris Froome sprints away to win stage seven at La Planche des Belles Filles.

RIGHT An ambition achieved as the yellow jersey is put on for the first time after stage seven.

> **'To be here, on the top of a mountain in the yellow jersey is phenomenal.'**
> – Wiggins after stage seven

idleness because they can't ever imagine applying themselves to do anything in their lives.

'It's easy for them to sit under a pseudonym on Twitter and write that sort of ****, rather than get off their arses in their own lives and apply themselves and work hard at something and achieve something. And that's ultimately it. *****.'

The inquisitor was astonished at the reaction; in the past, comments on the topic of doping were often banal. Not with Wiggins. Brailsford backed Wiggins, who received support from within and outside cycling for the sentiment expressed, including from controversial footballer Joey Barton and Rugby World Cup-winning coach Sir Clive Woodward, deputy *chef de mission* of the British Olympic team, although the language used was met with criticism from some quarters.

Another intriguing sub-plot was to follow as Froome moved into overall contention while Wiggins claimed a commanding first Tour stage success in the stage nine time-trial to Besançon. As leader, Wiggins was the last to roll down the start ramp and relished every revolution of the wheels. Sports director Sean Yates followed Wiggins in the Team Sky car and provided encouragement by reminding him of the sacrifices made in search of glory in Paris – missing his children's birthdays, sleeping in the spare room in an altitude tent 'like "ET"' – as he showed his supremacy against the clock.

Froome finished 35 seconds behind in second place on the stage as the Team Sky leader took a lead of one minute 53 seconds over second-placed Evans, ahead of the Tour's first rest day. Wiggins was far from complacent. 'It's never over until the fat lady sings and she hasn't entered the room yet,' he said. After moving into third place, Froome said: 'It's all for

RIGHT An outstanding time-trial to Besançon on stage nine opened up almost two minutes on Cadel Evans.

'Whatever happens, I am part of this team and always want to be part of it to the end of my career. I was the one given the role to lead the team at this year's Tour and I took the responsibility.'
– Wiggins on his commitment to Team Sky

Bradley at the moment.' Wiggins and his Team Sky colleagues went on a short ride, featuring a cafe stop, on the first rest day before relaxing at their two-star hotel amid the vineyards in Quincie-en-Beaujolais, where Wiggins was asked to pose for the next day's front page of French sportspaper *L'Equipe*, the official Tour diary.

Wiggins' lead remained intact on the Tour's first big mountains day, but he faced further questions on doping. Wiggins was asked to explain his outburst in Switzerland and gave a more rational reply. 'To me, it's them ******* all over everything I've done, by just saying "oh yes, he's cheating"', Wiggins said. 'There's one reason why I'm in this position and that's because I've worked hard. It's not like I've just come from nowhere.'

The questions were to become more challenging after the Tour's toughest mountain day, the 11th stage from Albertville, host city of the 1992 Winter Olympics, to La Toussuire, as Vincenzo Nibali, a rival for the overall title, attacked on the finishing ascent in a bid to eat into Wiggins' advantage.

Wiggins and Froome worked together to bridge the gap, with the *maillot jaune* doing much of the work himself as Evans was dropped. Froome then took to the front, with Wiggins on his wheel as the duo caught Nibali's group. Then Froome accelerated again, opening up a clear gap 4km from the finish, with Wiggins left behind. Froome looked over his shoulder, realised his yellow-clad team-mate was not with him and then reached for his race radio to establish where Wiggins was. The incident prompted immediate questions: was the attack planned? Who called Froome back? Was Wiggins unable to go with him? Or did he pull rank, believing the manoeuvre was unnecessary?

Wiggins suggested it was the latter, but the prospect of Froome attacking in the closing stages to try to claim second place from Evans had been discussed ahead of the start. Froome did attack in the final 500 metres, as planned, and Yates confirmed afterwards he halted the earlier move.

Team Sky were not about to set their leaders, separated by more than two minutes, against each other. 'It (the time gap) makes the roles clearer until the situation is otherwise,' Yates said. 'There is no point in gambling. We want to try and win the Tour, we don't want to spin the roulette wheel.' But had Froome's acceleration exposed a weakness in Wiggins' weaponry? Froome said: 'I'll follow orders at all costs. Our plan is to look after Bradley. He's just as strong as me, I think, and stronger than me in the time-trial.'

Debate raged, including on Twitter, where Froome's girlfriend and Wiggins' wife provided 140-character commentary. Some were hoping Froome would be set free and a battle royal would commence between team-mates, as with Bernard Hinault and Greg LeMond at the 1986 Tour. The Tour is so often won in the mountains and Froome had shown himself to be the leading climber in the race, but Team Sky knew the time-trials would be decisive on this occasion and that is Wiggins' domain. The British squad also believed in their leader's ability in the mountains. Speculation was sparked by the incident: surely Froome had to leave Team Sky? Would Wiggins support Froome in a more mountainous Tour in future? Wiggins was focused on the here and now, but insisted the team would always come first. He said: 'Whatever happens, I am part of this team and always want to be part of it to the end of my career. I was the one given the role to lead the team at this year's Tour and I took the responsibility. What is important is the team succeeds, otherwise there is no point in me being in the team if it's all about me. I am the face of it, but it's never just been about me.'

Wiggins had remained calm in the face of attacks from rivals and perceived attacks from team-mates and then had to fend off spectators on stage 12 to Annonay-Davézieux, won by

RIGHT Chris Froome's sudden burst on stage 11 proved to be one of the biggest talking points of the Tour.

Millar, who became the fourth British stage winner of the 99th Tour on the 45th anniversary of the death of Tom Simpson, Britain's first Tour leader. Near Sarras, 25km from the day's finish, over-exuberant spectators ran alongside the peloton, brandishing flares. Wiggins was struck. 'I'm covered in yellow stuff. It burnt my arm a bit,' he said.

After surviving that assault, Wiggins then faced further inquisition on the topic of doping in cycling, after addressing the issue himself in an online blog. Having previously felt he should not have to justify himself just because he was wearing the *maillot jaune*, Wiggins came to appreciate the need to better articulate his anti-doping stance. 'There's no point in me sitting and swearing every time that question gets asked,' he said. 'Perhaps I shouldn't take it personally, perhaps it's just a position our sport is in from people who have set a precedent, sat in this position before me. I do want to start building bridges to prove that I'm doing this off of bread and water and hard work and nothing else. If I can be as open, as honest as possible, hopefully that will go some way to people believing that what I'm doing is honest.' Wiggins emphasised what he had to lose – his reputation, his family – using the metaphor of a hand full of sand, which would slip through his fingers. The response was greeted with satisfaction from many, even by some of the most cynical observers who had witnessed the heart of the sport tainted by scandal after scandal. Others demanded to know more. Wiggins added: 'Sometimes I think for certain people whatever you do will never be enough unless they came and lived with me for 12 months, which I'm not prepared for them to do.'

Wiggins' reputation grew on stages 13 and 14 as his character shone through. There was the rare sight of the Tour leader playing a supporting role as the Briton attempted to set Edvald Boasson Hagen up for victory on the Bastille Day stage to Le Cap d'Agde. Wiggins powered to the front of the peloton in the final kilometre, with his Norwegian team-mate dragged along behind, before pulling away for Boasson Hagen to sprint ahead, only to be beaten into third place. 'It was the safest place to be,' said Wiggins. 'There was no extra exertion doing the lead-out and it was just nice to help Eddy, because I'd like to be able to pay him back in some way.' The following day, and a week before the Tour's conclusion in Paris, Wiggins featured in a *L'Equipe* cartoon, his profile made more distinctive by his sideburns being shaped into the outline of France. He also led the neutralisation of the peloton, less than 40km from the finish in Foix, following an incident of sabotage as carpet tacks were thrown on the road. A break was well clear, fighting for the stage win, with none of the leaders an overall threat. As the peloton crested the summit of the day's final climb, the Mur de Péguère, Evans punctured and saw his title defence unravelling. Wiggins realised something was amiss. 'So many guys punctured at once, it became quite apparent very quickly that something was up,' Wiggins said. 'It didn't seem the honourable thing to do, to benefit from other people's misfortune at a part of the race which was over.'

It is etiquette not to attack when another rider suffers a puncture or mechanical failure, and French television hailed Wiggins as 'Le Gentleman' afterwards for adhering to the amateur ethos of sportsmanship. The escapees appeared to survive the indiscriminate attack unscathed, but 61 punctures were caused to bikes, team cars and official vehicles.

As the Tour entered the final week and the decisive stages of the 99th race in the Pyrenees, Wiggins and Froome were asked further questions about their position in first and second place in the general classification. Wiggins gave short shrift to a suggestion Froome would be his greatest rival, if the pair were riding for different teams. He said: 'It doesn't take a rocket scientist to work that out. He's my team-mate. We'll keep it like that.' Froome meanwhile had to downplay comments attributed to him which suggested unhappiness with his position. He said: 'There's no bad blood in the team. We're still here with the same goal.'

Team Sky showed a united front on the Tour's second rest day, addressing the world's media on the sun-baked lawn of their Pau hotel. Wiggins' position in the standings was commanding and five-times Tour champion Miguel Indurain sent him a gift. The Spaniard, who Wiggins idolised while growing up in London, sent him a neckerchief he had worn for the Pamplona bull run, signed with a good luck message and embroidered with the crest of the local saint. Wiggins was aware of the significance of the gesture, but he was equally

LEFT Wiggins, Cavendish and Froome work for Sky team-mate Edvald Boasson Hagen as they head for the Med on stage 14.

BELOW LEFT Defending champion Cadel Evans was among those to suffer punctures on Mur de Péguère. Wiggins was hailed as 'Le Gentleman' for slowing the peloton.

BELOW An exhausted David Millar remains the focus of the media after becoming the fourth British stage winner on the 2012 Tour.

The peloton is dwarfed by the Pyrenean landscape on the Col D'Aubique on stage 16 between Pau and Bagnères de Luchon.

LEFT Edvald Boasson
Hagen leads Team Sky
down the Granier pass.

RIGHT Racing through
contrasting weather
conditions on the Croix de
Fer (top) and Port du Bales
(bottom).

aware there were potential pitfalls in each of the five remaining days of racing. Brailsford found it difficult to comprehend hypothetical questions about Paris, because there was still a race to be won. 'The closer you get, the more risk we have of the c-word,' said Brailsford, resulting in laughter from the British press pack, who remembered the expletives which marked Wiggins' first day in the yellow jersey all too well. Brailsford was referring to complacency. He need not have worried as Wiggins was not ready to picture himself in Paris. He retained his day-to-day approach, but he was prepared to answer the hypothetical questions, the questions about his background and history – and those about Froome. Wiggins said: 'What we do well is we race as a team. That's why we're in this position now. I am surrounded by incredibly talented bike riders – including Chris Froome. The guy is capable of winning the Tour, for sure, otherwise he wouldn't be second overall, and he will win this race one day and I will be there to support him doing that. People will try to make more of a story than it is, but we've gone out there each day and proved on the road that there isn't a problem.' Froome's support was to be integral on the next two Pyrenean days.

Wiggins survived repeated attacks on the 16th stage to Bagnères-de-Luchon, with Nibali leading the assault without wounding his rival. The Italian all but conceded defeat afterwards. 'Sky were too strong today. I'm aiming for the podium,' Nibali said. 'It's getting too hard to open the door.'

The door was firmly closed to Evans, who suffered again, losing more than four minutes to his rivals. The Australian said: 'That's pretty much the Tour de France over for me.'

Wiggins was having none of it. He said: 'I don't think that the others have eased up trying to beat me and start thinking of the other places on the podium. Not yet.'

One big mountain day remained and it was the last chance for rivals to claim significant gains on Wiggins, the supreme time-triallist in the field. The 17th stage to Peyragudes was a brute, with the Port de Bales to negotiate before the Col de Peyresourde, which formed part of the summit finish. If anyone was going to beat Wiggins they had to attack there. Instead of defending himself under an onslaught of attacks, Wiggins found himself teary-eyed as he crested the summit of the Peyresourde alone with Froome, who was seen beckoning his leader to stick with him. Froome's gesticulating in the closing kilometres as he finished second to Alejandro Valverde was interpreted by some as an act which again showed his superiority in the mountains, but as Wiggins subsequently explained, his team-mate was merely urging him to focus.

Wiggins said: 'That moment I went over with Chris, all the fight went out of the window, everything to do with the performance. At that point, the first time in this whole Tour since I've led this race, I thought "maybe I've just won the Tour". And that's when it starts getting hard then because you lose concentration. It was an incredible feeling. It really was.'

Froome helped Wiggins, who had not fallen out of the top two in the whole race since finishing second to Cancellara in the prologue, gain valuable seconds over Nibali and consolidated his own position in second place.

For the first time in his imperious season, Wiggins had victory in Paris on his mind and within his grasp. Yet still his achievement was not fully recognised by some, due to the absences of the banned Alberto Contador and injured Andy Schleck. 'No-one's actually patted me on the back yet, it's all still in a negative sense,' he said. Unbeknown to him, the British media were lauding Wiggins for moving on the verge of history as thousands of people prepared to cross the Channel for the Tour's final weekend to acclaim a new national hero.

Wiggins was not finished yet. On the face of it, the final three stages to the Champs-Elysées, including the time-trial, appeared to be a procession. Wiggins was taking nothing for granted and was determined to do his bit to repay the support of his team-mates and one man in particular. Cavendish signed for Team Sky believing a bid for the yellow jersey and the points classification green jersey he won in 2011 was

possible, but ended up playing a peripheral role in his first Tour with the British team.

The Manxman was been stuffing bottles and rain capes up his world champion's rainbow jersey in an unaccustomed role working as a *domestique* in the service of Wiggins. On the Team Sky bus prior to the 18th stage to Brive-la-Gaillarde, Cavendish pleaded for an opportunity, but Yates was keen his riders conserved energy after two arduous days in the mountains. Wiggins butted in and made the call – he was keen to reward Cavendish. Cavendish was honoured to be part of a team on the verge of history, but was desperate for his chance to win another stage and he delivered. Afterwards he said: 'It's like Wayne Rooney playing in defence. You can still win a match, but you can't do your part of that to the best of your ability. Today we set it up and we scored the goal.'

If Cavendish was the scorer, the assist fell to Wiggins, whose scintillating pace gobbled up the day's late escape before Cavendish skilfully negotiated the finale to win. Wiggins fulfilled another ambition by helping his friend to a stage success and punched the air with delight as Cavendish finished arms aloft in the Tour for the 22nd time. 'He's been an incredible team-mate the last couple of weeks,' Wiggins said. 'It's nice to be able to pay him back. It's been hard every morning, thinking about the GC and maybe sacrificing some sprint stages. Nine times out of 10 Cav finishes it off when you do something like that. And once again he showed, if there was any doubt, that he is the fastest man in the world.'

It was then Wiggins' turn to show his supreme talent and solidify his hold on the yellow jersey in the penultimate day's race against the clock. He did so with élan and with thousands waving Union flags lining the route south-west of Paris. Wiggins claimed an imperious victory, with Froome second, more than one minute behind, to go more than three minutes clear of the field entering the final day's procession to Paris. It was as if Wiggins was making a point to those suggesting Froome should have been Team Sky's leader. For Wiggins, it was the culmination of a lifelong dream. 'It doesn't get much bigger than this,' he said. 'You couldn't write a better script. What a way to finish. I just wanted to finish the job off in style. There was a lot of emotion in the last 10k. Everything was going through my mind. All the years of getting to this point, my family, disappointments, crashing out the Tour last year, watching Cadel in this very position a year ago in Grenoble. I always imagined what that would feel like and now I know. I really wanted to get out there and finish with a bang. Fortunately I managed to do that.'

Team Sky's blue livery transformed into yellow overnight – something Brailsford did not approve of, with the race officially still to be won – and Wiggins' bike, which had become progressively more yellow in the final week, was now one colour. As with all fine pieces of theatre, Wiggins' victorious Tour was to have a grand finale. Most previous Tour leaders have been content to enjoy the ceremonial final stage to the Champs-Elysées, contested by the sprinters, but

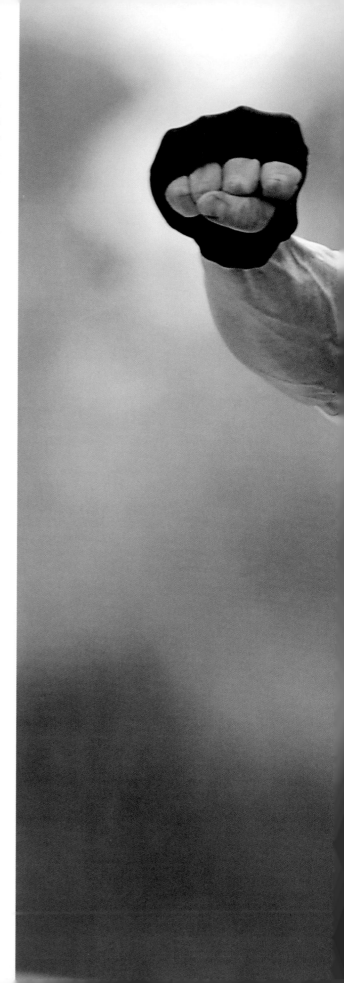

Another time-trial and another scintillating performance ensures Wiggins wears the yellow jersey into Paris.

LEFT The spine-tingling sight of the *maillot jaune* leading out the world champion's rainbow jersey – both worn by British riders – on the Champs-Elysées in Paris.

ABOVE Team Sky's tactics pay off handsomely as Cavendish celebrates winning the final stage in Paris for the fourth time.

RIGHT Together to the end – Team Sky riders gather in Paris.

'We're just going to draw the raffle numbers now.'
– Wiggins' now famous remark on the podium

Wiggins wanted to play a full part in the frantic finale on the cobbles of the French capital's most famous boulevard. Cavendish was seeking a fourth successive win on the final stage, and, just as in Brive, Wiggins was determined to make it happen. The sight of the yellow jersey leading out the world champion in one of the greatest arenas of sport was something to behold; the fact the duo were British left the travelling fans in raptures. Wiggins said: 'Every lap of the Champs-Elysées was goose-pimple stuff. For Mark to finish it off like that, well, it couldn't get any better.'

After standing on the top step of the podium, Wiggins was asked to address the crowd and the worldwide television audience. 'We're just going to draw the raffle numbers now,' he cheekily joked.

'Thanks for the amazing support the last three weeks. I really appreciate it. It's been a magical couple of weeks. Some dreams do come true. My old mother over there, her son's just won the Tour de France. Thank you everyone. Cheers. Have a safe journey home and don't get too drunk.'

Wiggins savoured his success, rolling over the cobbles with his seven-year-old son Ben riding alongside in a scaled-down version of his dad's bike. Despite his achievement, Wiggins had to forgo the usual Paris party and spurned even handshakes from old friends for fear of catching a cold. 'I've got an Olympics to go and win,' he said. And with that, Wiggins departed Paris on a private jet to return to the UK and seek further success.

FAR RIGHT Celebrating with wife Cath on the Champs-Elysées in Paris.

RIGHT Reunited with children Isabella and Ben.

ABOVE RIGHT A replica bike was waiting in Paris for Ben to join in the celebrations.

Le TOUR de FRANCE 2012

Lesley Garrett sings the national anthem for the two British riders on the podium. Vincenzo Nibali (right) makes up the top three.

On the podium at Hampton Court Palace, flanked by silver medallist Tony Martin (left) and third-placed Chris Froome.

THE KING'S PALACE

The front and back pages of the newspapers on July 23, 2012, the Monday before the London Olympics opened, were adorned with photographs of Bradley Wiggins winning the Tour de France. Wiggins was already well known in cycling circles, but now he was a household name and an inspiration, even to his team-mates ahead of a home Games.

British Cycling performance director Dave Brailsford said: 'I walked into Newport, where the track team are, and they were all just buzzing from it. Chris Hoy, Vicky (Pendleton), all the team pursuit teams, they were absolutely on a high from it. It's difficult to measure, but it's certainly given the whole team a lift.'

For the vast majority of people, once a lifelong ambition is attained, there is a moment to pause and reflect. Wiggins returned from Paris to his home in Chorley to spend two nights with his wife Cath and children, Isabella and Ben, but did not rest. Television crews and photographers followed, desperate for pictures and a snatched word with Britain's new hero, training in the lanes of Lancashire. The goldfish bowl-like existence of the Tour had shielded Wiggins from the euphoria of his success, an achievement which had transcended sport. A letter from the Queen arrived but Wiggins was just as happy with direct Twitter messages from Smiths guitarist Johnny Marr and ex-Liverpool striker Robbie Fowler. 'I had a message from God,' Liverpool fan Wiggins said. 'It's been overwhelming. I never realised or imagined it would be this big, how much it would reach out to the general public.'

Wiggins, a self-styled recluse, craved normality, but he was keen to keep the momentum of his Tour triumph going until the Olympic time-trial at Hampton Court Palace. The Olympic Games, in his home city, was a means of keeping his focus post-Tour. He said: 'Normally you would have a week off the bike, but with the Olympics we've had to keep going; do all the usual stuff as if it's a continuation of the Tour. It's been a good way to try to soak up what's happened in the last few weeks. With the focus of the Olympics it's been a good excuse to get down to what you do best, which is riding your bike.'

The London 2012 road events were to take place in Surrey and the British squad were housed in a luxury hotel used to welcoming the Premier League's top footballers, but now with new stars among their guests. The country club surroundings contrasted with the low-rated Tour hotels and the athletes'

village in east London, but the presence of his team-mates and British Cycling's head of logistics, Doug Dailey, reminded Wiggins he was at the Games. He said: 'It's odd being at the Olympics in London. It definitely feels like the Olympics, because wherever Doug is you know it's an Olympic thing. I only ever see Doug every four years, since Sydney; every four years he says "you've done a bit better since the last time I saw you". It's like Doug's been there through my whole career.' Wiggins, in his fourth Games, was part of Mark Cavendish's 'dream team' alongside David Millar, Chris Froome and Ian Stannard, seeking to deliver the Manxman to a first Olympic title in the road race. Wiggins and Cavendish had Olympic history following their Madison disappointment and post-Beijing fall-out in 2008, but Wiggins dismissed making amends for that failure as motivation. Copenhagen, Brive and the Champs-Elysées had atoned for that. 'I think I've repaid

LEFT Relaxing on a golden throne and reflecting on a job well done.

ABOVE A brief visit home offered no respite from the photographers' lenses.

'This is what Cav has been living for for most of the year. He's been there for me the last month and now he can sense that it's his turn and we're all there for him.'
– Wiggins on the Olympic road race

that at the worlds last year, that lap I did, and at the Tour, leading him out in the yellow jersey – it doesn't get much better than that,' Wiggins said.

Wiggins was happy to hand the leadership mantle over to Cavendish, who had focused his season on the 250-kilometre route through Surrey, featuring nine ascents of Box Hill. 'This is what Cav has been living for for most of the year,' Wiggins said. 'He's looking as fit as I've ever seen him on the bike and we're approaching the thing he's been thinking about since he won the world title. He's been there for me the last month and now he can sense that it's his turn and we're all there for him.'

Wiggins' Olympic priority was the time-trial on day five of the Games and he had initially considered not completing the 250km road race. But following his time-trial performance on the penultimate day of the Tour in Chartres, there was no doubt in his mind he could fulfil team duties before focusing on his personal goal. He said: 'I've just done a world-class time-trial, averaging a ridiculous amount of power, after three weeks' bike racing and two really tough Pyrenees stages, a 222km stage at 44kph average speed with a lead-out in the final (in Brive). Once you start thinking in those terms, that you're so fit and you've trained for the demands of the three weeks and you've actually got three days off in between the road race and the time-trial, it shouldn't be a problem. If anything, I'm going to be fresher.'

Wiggins was in action on the first full day of competition, with the public expectation that he would help Cavendish become the first British champion of London 2012. As a result of the schedule, the riders missed marching at the opening ceremony, a showcase of Britishness. Wiggins, though, was given a role, starting proceedings by ringing the largest harmonically-tuned bell in the world, while wearing a yellow jersey. Little more than 12 hours later, the day dawned brightly and the 'dream team' assembled on the start line on The Mall to be introduced to the crowd and Prince Charles and his wife the Duchess of Cornwall, who live at nearby St James' Palace.

RIGHT Wiggins rang a giant bell in the Olympic Stadium to signal the start of the London 2012 opening ceremony.

BELOW Working at the head of the peloton for road race team-mate Mark Cavendish proved ultimately to be in vain.

Wiggins might have cracked a joke – 'they only popped out for a newspaper and a pint of milk' – but instead focused on the task at hand, reminding rival teams that Britain had 'the fastest man in the world' in their ranks. In being granted a royal reception, it was as if Cavendish was being proclaimed champion even before the race began. But he and his team-mates knew the size of the challenge that faced them as they attempted to set up a sprint for the Manxman. More than a million people lined the route, some adopting the Tour mentality and sleeping in campervans, keen to capture a glimpse of Wiggins and Cavendish. Wiggins led by example, riding on the front of the peloton for the majority of the race, but Britain and Cavendish missed the crucial break on the final ascent of Box Hill. A sprint for Cavendish was 'plan A and the rest of the alphabet', as Brailsford put it, and the hunt began, but the size of the escape and talent within the group meant a successful chase was beyond even Wiggins and the most talented squad assembled for an Olympic road race. Realising the chase was up before The Mall was in sight, Wiggins sat up before Cavendish finished 29th as Alexandre Vinokourov won. Wiggins immediately refocused on the time-trial and returned to Surrey to hone his preparations, including inspecting the 44km route closely for the first time. Wiggins had the backing of his team-mates after their quest to deliver victory for Cavendish ended. Millar said: 'Brad against the world when they're all on their own, he can wrap that up. He's got such incredible form and he's in such good spirits. I think we'll get our gold medal there.'

Wiggins had spoken of the calm serenity of the surroundings in Surrey, where security ensured he was not like a 'monkey in a cage' and photographed eating his breakfast, as at the Tour, but he did report a theft to his Twitter followers. He had left his training kit in an unlocked locker while taking a sauna at the hotel's spa and returned to find it missing. The incident provoked a minor storm, with the hotel releasing two statements. 'It seems an overzealous fan has scored a fantastic London 2012 souvenir,' said the first, before a clarification insisting they did not condone theft. Wiggins wrote on Twitter: 'Gotta delete tweet Re the thief, bad PR, never mind my kit though.' For Wiggins it was no more than a minute distraction from the task at hand – adding to his haul of three gold and six Olympic medals in all.

'Brad against the world when they're all on their own, he can wrap that up. I think we'll get our gold medal there.'
– David Millar, Wiggins' team-mate

RIGHT The Tour de France is temporarily forgotten and Olympic gold is Wiggins' sole focus at London 2012.

More than a million spectators lined the route of the
Olympic time-trial in south-west London.

> **'The Tour is such a good boot camp for this. So an hour time-trial to make history should be a doddle.'**
> – Wiggins on his bid for a seventh medal

On the final day of the Tour, Wiggins spoke of 'gold or nothing' in the time-trial, and in Surrey he was confident of improving his season-long unbeaten record in lengthy races against the clock. 'The Tour is such a good boot camp for this,' said Wiggins. 'This is going be a piece of **** now compared to that. It's just an hour and not three weeks. That's the baseline of worst-case scenario of pressure and expectation, with three weeks lying ahead of you. And we handled that pretty well, so an hour time-trial to make history should be a doddle.'

The history of which Wiggins was speaking was becoming the Briton with the most Olympic medals; he was level with rower Sir Steve Redgrave before the time-trial's start at Henry VIII's Hampton Court Palace, with the same number of medals as the king had wives. But there was added expectation – day five of the Olympics, Wednesday, August 1, 2012, had arrived with Britain still seeking its first gold of the home Games. The full glare of expectation returned to Wiggins, with one tabloid newspaper producing the outline of his hair and sideburns for readers to cut out and wear, accompanied with the headline 'Here Wiggo' on the front page. Another had cut-out-and-keep golden sideburns in honour of his quest for glory, with headlines reading 'Going for Wiggold' and 'Golden Burns'. Another newspaper produced a poster, illustrated with the Royal Air Force roundel, a symbol adopted by Mods, and Wiggins. 'Keep calm and carry on,' it read. 'We've still got Wiggo.' There was a hashtag on Twitter, adopted by those showing their support in 140 characters. Cath Wiggins, his wife, wrote: '#wiggowednesday apparently. No pressure then!' But for once, Wiggins was beaten to it as, at the Eton Dorney rowing lake, around 20 miles from the streets where he was

'Normally you say "I've won three golds", never "a silver and two bronze". There was only one colour today. The most important statistic is number four for me and not number seven.'
– Wiggins on his fourth Olympic gold medal

RIGHT Celebration time with wife Cath and then performance director Dave Brailsford (far right).

BELOW Ecstatic fans hail Great Britain's second gold medal of the Games.

seeking gold, rowers Heather Stanning and Helen Glover claimed a convincing win in the women's pairs.

Wiggins was not to be outdone as he rolled down the start ramp seeking another piece of history. The time-trial was his domain and he adopted the still upper body position, legs pumping like pistons, he had used thousands of times before. An imperious performance saw Wiggins complete the route less than 51 minutes later and, with a partisan din ringing in his ears, he collected a fourth Olympic title.

He waited for Fabian Cancellara, the 2008 time-trial champion, to cross the finish line before beginning his celebrations by remounting his bike and returning down the route. 'I wanted to go and see my wife and all the people that had come to stand there on the roadside,' he said. 'We all know about the Olympic ticketing. The great thing about cycling is it's free to come and watch. It's a bit of a prawn-sandwich fest (in the ticketed area). Ultimately all the real fans are out there. It's nice to go back out the gates and just appreciate everything they did. It was nice to go back out, roll up and down.' Wiggins fondly recalled the wall of noise which accompanied every revolution of his pedals, particularly entering and exiting a roundabout in Kingston, and which propelled him to glory and greatness.

Wiggins, typically, was reluctant to discuss the issue of greatness or the prospect of following Redgrave and Sir Chris Hoy in receiving a knighthood. He said: 'To be mentioned in the same breath as people like Steve Redgrave and Chris Hoy is an honour. Ultimately it's all about the gold medals once you've been Olympic champion. The other ones, you don't really talk about them. When somebody says "how many medals have you won at the Olympics?" Normally you say "I've won three golds", never "a silver and two bronze". There was only one colour today. The most important statistic is number four for me and not number seven.'

Asked 'How does Sir Wiggo sound to you?' he said: 'It doesn't quite sound right, let's be honest. As much as an honour it

RIGHT A huge reception on a trip to support team-mates at the London 2012 Velodrome.

OPPOSITE Meeting music legend Paul Weller, hero and Modfather.

would be to receive something like that, I don't think I'd ever use it. I'd just put it in a drawer. I'll always just be Brad.'

As the national anthem was being played and bright sunlight lifted the gloom of a day which started in overcast conditions, Wiggins' achievements began to sink in. 'There is almost slight melancholy,' he said. 'I realised on the podium that that's probably it for me. I don't think anything is going to top that; winning the Tour and then winning Olympic gold in London. To go out there today and put a performance like that together nine days after the Tour and win another Olympic title in another event, it is never, ever going to get any better than that. It's been an amazing six weeks. This was the plan. I've answered all the questions in the last six weeks. We've done it.' The collective referred to the team, for although Wiggins was an individual champion, he recognised the support of his fellow riders, coaches and support staff.

Brailsford's role could not be underestimated, but the Welshman preferred to talk up his rider as the best British Olympian of them all. 'Bradley now deserves to be recognised,' Brailsford said. 'I'd be biased, of course, and I think the difference between what Bradley's done and anybody else is that he's done them in different disciplines, whereas everybody else has done it in similar disciplines. If you can go from the track – individual pursuit, team pursuit and Madison – and then do it in the road time-trial, I don't think anybody can touch that.' His performance left his compatriots and rivals purring. Brailsford said: 'To pull off a performance like that off the back of what he's been through over the last few weeks is – phew – off the scale.' Germany's Tony Martin, who beat Wiggins to the world title in 2011, had to settle for Olympic silver and described the Briton as 'unbeatable'. Cancellara, for

so long the leading rider against the clock, added to the praise, saying: 'He had his perfect ride today. He's on another level.'

As if to again illustrate the range of his talents, Wiggins floated the prospect of a track return for the Rio de Janeiro Olympics in 2016, at the age of 36. He said: 'I could envisage, depending on what my wife thinks, going back to the track in the team pursuit where it all started and trying to win a fifth. But that's a long way off.'

With his London 2012 Games complete, Wiggins' thoughts turned to the velodrome, which was set to begin the following day. It was the first Olympics when he would not grace the Siberian pine of the velodrome after his favoured event, the 4km individual pursuit, was dropped from the programme. He was keen to see his friends and former team-mates in action. As for the longer-term future Wiggins was uncertain. 'You train all year for the physical aspect, to try and get the results; you can't train or plan for what comes next,' he said. 'I don't know what comes next. External perception might change, but inside you're still the same person. You want to go back to normal life. Whether that happens or not is a different thing. You just deal with it as you go along – it's why people end up in The Priory, I guess. I'm glad it's over. I've lived for August 1 for nine months knowing it was all going to be over and I could go and have a vodka-tonic. It's here now. It's done and I've won the Tour and I've won the Olympics, Paris-Nice and all those other races.'

The vodka-tonics soon flowed, toasting an epic adventure, culminating in two historic triumphs. He partied in a roof-top bar overlooking the dome of St Paul's Cathedral and attended a secret Stone Roses concert, where he chatted with his idol Paul Weller. Photographers clamoured for pictures of Wiggins

'I'm glad it's over. I've lived for August 1 for nine months knowing it was all going to be over and I could go and have a vodka-tonic. It's here now.'
– Wiggins after the Olympic time-trial

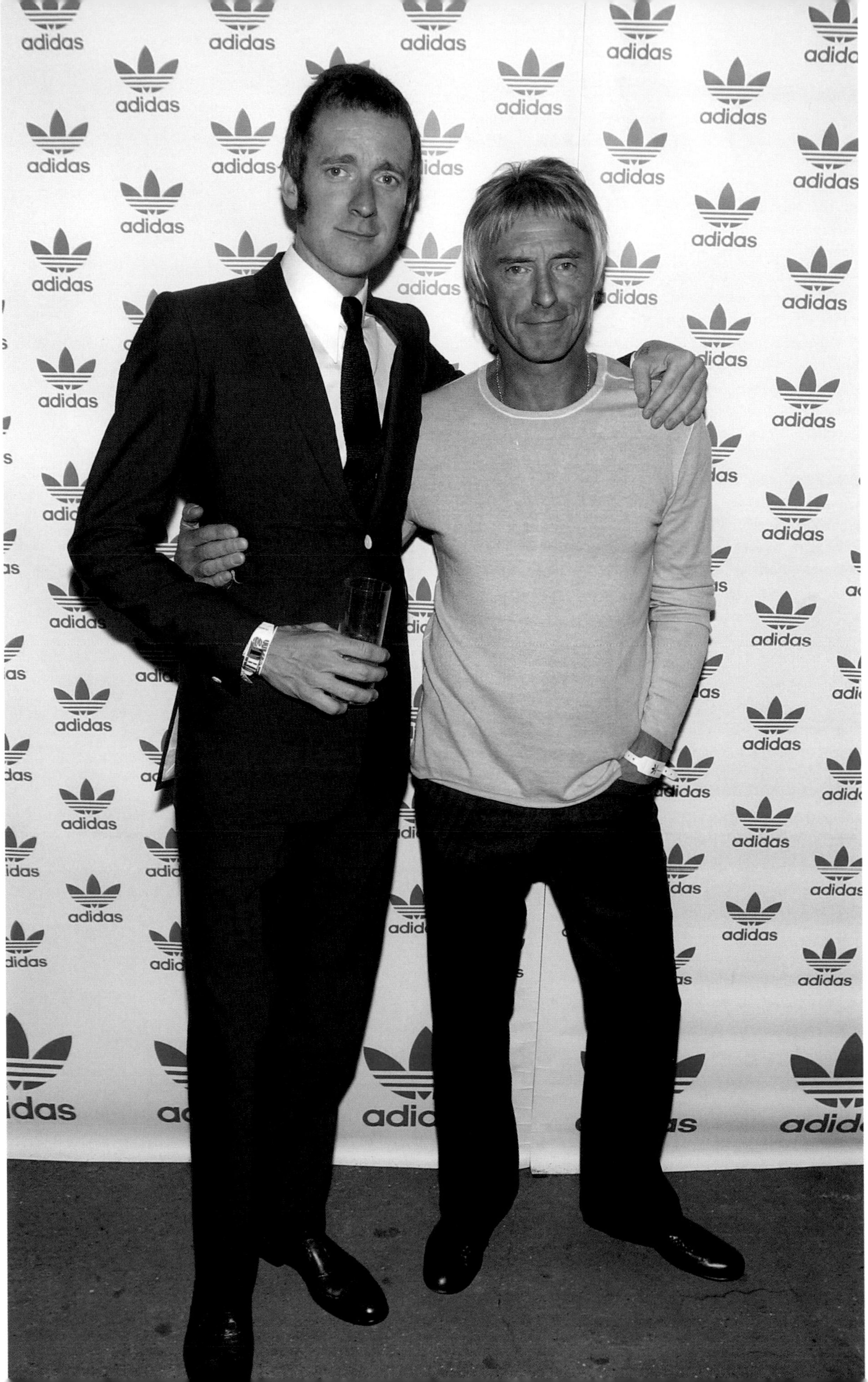
adidas

with a drink in hand, but he provided one himself in his own style, making a victory sign. He wrote on Twitter: 'Well what a day, blind drunk at the minute and overwhelmed with all the messages, Thank You everyone it's been emotional X.'

Still the scale of his achievement was taking a while to sink in. He said: 'It's all a bit strange. I'm used to being Olympic champion and the satisfaction of winning a fourth gold is an honour in itself. I've got to keep reminding myself I won the Tour a couple of weeks ago. It's a bit overwhelming, a bit like Christmas day being a kid with all these presents – I don't know which one to play with.'

Much of Wiggins' joy came from witnessing others revelling in his success. 'It's been phenomenal and ultimately what the Olympics are about,' he added. 'Seeing how many people went away happy to the bars, it was like a football match where people continued celebrating into the night. Thinking you've done that, helping people have a nice afternoon and evening is very satisfying. I've inspired some people and that's brilliant – that's ultimately what we're all about – and I've made a lot of people happy, which is humbling.'

Wiggins was soon craving normality, the school run and supermarket shopping. 'One thing I am quite adamant about is things aren't going to change too much,' he said. 'I train hard, I work hard. Ultimately I am very normal in my life, aside from cycling. I'm not a celebrity, I will never be a celebrity. I despise that whole celebrity culture. I left home six weeks ago for the Tour de France, known in cycling circles, but a relative no-one to the general public. A lot's changed. I'm grateful for everything, the attention and the adulation, because I have a lot of appreciation for what people achieve in sport and I have a lot of heroes and people I idolise in sport for what they've achieved. To just be up there and be looked upon as inspiring or whatever is brilliant.' He was also becoming more accustomed to the questions of a knighthood, changing his mind to say: 'Sir Wiggo sounds nice.'

Only a few miles from where he grew up, to a single mum and an absent father, the 'Kid from Kilburn' was now a national hero. He said: 'I'm just trying to soak it all up now. We'll go on to try to achieve more stuff now but I don't think I'm ever going to top winning a home Olympics on the roads of London. Not many people get an opportunity to do that and it's brilliant.'

'We'll go on to try to achieve more stuff now but I don't think I'm ever going to top winning a home Olympics.'
– Wiggins reflects on a career highlight

RIGHT On stage to receive a rapturous welcome from fans at the BT London Live event in Hyde Park.

CHORLEY & LEYLAND
Guardian
chorley-guardian.co.uk
THURSDAY
FREEDOM
OF CHORLEY
FOR
WIGGINS
LANCASHIRE
Evening Post
lep.co.uk
125

LEFT After unprecedented
success in the summer
of 2012, everyone loved
Bradley Wiggins.

TIMELINE AND RESULTS

1980 Born April 28 in Ghent, Belgium before growing up in London. Son of Australian former racing cyclist Gary Wiggins.

1992 Begins track cycling at Herne Hill Velodrome, London.

1997 Wins individual pursuit gold at Junior World Track Championships in Cuba.

2000
March Silver in team pursuit at Track Cycling World Championships in Manchester.

October Bronze in team pursuit at Olympic Games in Sydney.

2001
September Silver in team pursuit at Track Cycling World Championships in Antwerp, Belgium.

2002
July Silver for England in team pursuit and individual pursuit at Commonwealth Games in Manchester. Gold in individual pursuit at Track Cycling World Championships in Stuttgart, Germany.

2003
August Silver in team pursuit at Track Cycling World Championships in Stuttgart, Germany.

September Wins opening stage of Tour de l'Avenir.

2004
August Olympic gold in individual pursuit at Athens Olympics. Also wins silver in team pursuit alongside Steve Cummings, Paul Manning and Rob Hayles and bronze in the Madison alongside Rob Hayles to become the first British athlete since 1964 to win three medals at a single Olympic Games.

2005
September Wins stage eight of Tour de l'Avenir.

2006
July Makes Tour de France debut, riding for French team Cofidis.

2007
March Wins gold in both the individual pursuit and team pursuit at Track Cycling World Championships in Palma, Majorca.

June Prologue victory in Dauphiné Liberé.

July Finishes fourth in Tour de France prologue in London behind Swiss winner Fabian Cancellara but his team, Cofidis, later withdraw after teammate Cristian Moreni fails a drugs test.

2008
January Wiggins' estranged father, Gary Wiggins, is discovered unconscious in New South Wales and later dies.

March Wins individual pursuit, team pursuit and Madison gold at Track Cycling World Championships in Manchester.

August 16 Successfully defends Olympic individual pursuit title with gold at the Laoshan Velodrome.

GRAND TOUR RECORD
Tour de France
2012	Winner, won stages nine and 19
2011	Crashed out on stage seven
2010	23rd
2009	Fourth
2007	Combativity award, stage six, team withdrawn after stage 16
2006	124th

Vuelta a España
2011	Third

Giro d'Italia
2010	40th, won prologue
2009	71st
2008	134th
2005	123rd
2003	Eliminated after missing time limit on stage 18

OTHER MAJOR ROAD RACE RESULTS
Critérium du Dauphiné
2012	Winner, won stage four
2011	Winner
2007	95th, won prologue

Paris-Nice
2012	Winner, won stage eight
2011	Third

Tour de Romandie
2012	Winner, won stages one and five

OLYMPIC GAMES RECORD
London 2012	Gold, road time trial
Beijing 2008	Gold, individual pursuit
	Gold, team pursuit
Athens 2004	Gold, individual pursuit
	Silver, team pursuit
	Bronze, Madison
Sydney 2000	Bronze, team pursuit

COMMONWEALTH GAMES RECORD
Manchester 2002	Silver, individual pursuit
	Silver, team pursuit
Kuala Lumpur 1998	Silver, team pursuit

August 18 Olympic team pursuit gold alongside Ed Clancy, Geraint Thomas and Paul Manning in a world record of three minutes 53.314 seconds.

August 19 Favourite for Olympic Madison alongside Mark Cavendish but ninth-placed finish results in Manxman suffering the ignominy of being the only member of GB's track team to leave the Laoshan Velodrome without a medal and having a public falling-out with Wiggins.

2009
July Secures fourth place in Tour de France, matching highest-ever placing by a British rider.

September Wins British Time-Trial Championship.

October Wins stage five time-trial and overall title at Jayco Herald Sun Tour in Australia.

December Signs four-year deal with Team Sky, the BSkyB-backed road team which is being led by British Cycling performance director Dave Brailsford.

2010
February 7 Makes Team Sky debut at Tour of Qatar, helping squad win the race's opening team time-trial.

March Finishes third overall in the Tour of Murcia.

May Wins the Giro d'Italia prologue to become only the second Briton ever to wear the race leader's pink jersey (*maglia rosa*). The victory gives Team Sky a Grand Tour stage win at the first attempt.

July Finishes 24th on Team Sky's Tour de France debut, a position later upgraded to 23rd after Alberto Contador is stripped of the title for a doping offence.

2011
March Finishes third overall in Paris-Nice stage race.

May Wins fourth stage of Bayern-Rundfahrt as team-mate Geraint Thomas wins overall.

June Wins traditional Tour de France warm-up Critérium du Dauphiné. Wins British Championships road race.

July 8 Abandons Tour de France after fracturing collarbone in crash on seventh stage. Wiggins was sixth overall, 10 seconds behind race leader Thor Hushovd, entering the stage.

ABOVE Wiggins leads from the front for Team GB in the London 2012 Olympics road race.

WORLD CHAMPIONSHIPS

2011	**UCI Road World Championships** Silver, individual-time trial
2008	**UCI Track World Championships** Gold, individual pursuit Gold, team pursuit (world record time) Gold, Madison
2007	**UCI Track World Championships** Gold, individual pursuit Gold, team pursuit
2003	**UCI Track World Championships** Gold, individual pursuit Silver, team pursuit
2002	**UCI Track World Championships** Bronze, team pursuit
2001	**UCI Track World Championships** Silver, team pursuit
2000	**UCI Track World Championships** Silver, team pursuit
1997	**UCI Junior Track World Championships** Gold, individual pursuit

PROFESSIONAL TEAMS

2010-	Team Sky
2009	Garmin-Slipstream
2008	Team Highroad/Columbia
2006-2007	Cofidis
2004-2005	Crédit Agricole
2002-2003	Française des Jeux
2001	Linda McCartney Racing Team

September — Finishes third overall at the Vuelta a España. Finishes second in World Championships time-trial before helping Cavendish win the road race.

2012

February — Wins stage five of Volta ao Algarve.

March — Wins Paris-Nice overall.

April — Triumphs in Tour de Romandie, winning stages one and five.

June — Successfully defends his Critérium du Dauphiné title and wins stage four time-trial.

July 7 — Takes Tour de France yellow jersey after stage seven.

July 9 — Enhances hold on the *maillot jaune* with a first Tour stage win on the stage nine time-trial.

July 21 — Wins the time-trial on the Tour's penultimate day to all but secure victory.

July 22 — Confirmed as Britain's first-ever winner of the Tour de France.

August 1 — Claims gold medal for Team GB in Olympic road time-trial.

ACKNOWLEDGEMENTS

126

ABOVE Bradley Wiggins fulfils his childhood dream by winning the 2012 Tour de France.

About the Author
Matt McGeehan is a sports reporter for the Press Association, the UK's national news agency. Matt has covered four Track Cycling World Championships, three Tours de France and the London 2012 Olympic and Paralympic Games and interviewed Bradley Wiggins on track and road.

For the Press Association
Chris Wiltshire, News and Sports Editor
Mark Tattersall, Senior Sub-Editor

Picture Credits
All photographs © PRESS ASSOCIATION IMAGES except the following: Getty Images/Doug Pensinger: 21; Getty Images/Mike Powell: 18-19; Rex Features/Offside: 10-11, 12, 15 left, 15 right